GW00363644

What does it mean to be one?

A practical guide to child development in the Early Years Foundation Stage

Jennie Lindon

Contents

Published by Practical Pre-School Books
St Jude's Church, Dulwich Road, Herne Hill, London, SE24 0PB Tel. 020 7738 5454
© MA Education 2009
www.practicalpreschoolbooks.com

What does it mean to be one? ISBN: 978 1 90457 586 3

Focus on one-year-olds

What Does it Mean to be One? explores the developmental needs and likely skills of babies and young toddlers. This book is part of a series that considers a year at a time in the life of very young children. This title now takes the series into the very beginning of early childhood and links closely with *What does it mean to be two?* The approach and ideas of this book are relevant to any practitioners, working with babies and toddlers anywhere in the UK. The structure of the book, however, follows the framework for England of the Early Years Foundation Stage: guidance covering from birth to five years of age that became statutory for early years provision from September 2008.

Children's learning can only be effectively and appropriately supported when adults – practitioners and parents alike – are guided by sound knowledge of child development. The layout of each of the five books in this linked series includes:

- Descriptive developmental information within the main text, organised within the six areas of learning used by the Early Years Foundation Stage.
- 'For example' sections giving instances of real children and real places and sometimes references to useful sources of further examples.
- 'Being a helpful adult' boxes which focus on adult behaviour that is an effective support for children's learning, as well as approaches that could undermine young children.
- 'Food for thought' headings which highlight points of good practice in ways that can encourage reflection and discussion among practitioners, as well as sharing in partnership with parents.

Where are the ones in terms of early years provision?

This book covers the baby year up to the first birthday and into the year in which toddlers are one. A huge amount happens developmentally over this time span and some babies and toddlers will remain the full responsibility of their own family: parents or other adult family members. However, over the first part of very early childhood, some babies and toddlers will experience the transition into some kind of non-family care, for part or all of their week.

- Some of this age group will be cared for by somebody other than their parents, but within a family home: by a nanny employed by the family to work in their home or with a childminder who is based in her, or occasionally his, own family home.
- Other under ones and ones spend time in a group setting: a day nursery or a children's centre. Unless the setting is very small, the under twos (often under threes) are likely to be in a separate base room from the over threes.

Up to 2002 all national guidance across the UK was focussed on the over threes. England, Scotland and Wales each had their own early years curriculum document to guide practitioners working with three- to five-year-olds. The framework for Northern Ireland covered three- and four-year-olds, since young children start primary school in the September of the school year after their fourth birthday. Any guidance about good practice with under threes was developed within a local area by early years teams who were concerned about guiding or enhancing the quality of provision. Then, in 2002 the Birth to Three Matters framework was introduced in England, and in 2005 Scotland launched their *Birth to Three: Supporting our Youngest Children* framework.

The most recent changes are that:

- In England from September 2008 the birth to five Early Years Foundation Stage (EYFS) has replaced both the under-threes *Birth to Three Matters*, and the Foundation Stage for three-to five-year-old.
- In Scotland, the current developments for change revolve around a Curriculum for Excellence set to cover all children from three to eighteen years of age. In the earlier years, the main focus for development is for a continuity of more active learning and play from the early education of three-to five-year-olds into the first years of primary school. The Scottish birth to three guidance remains the framework for good practice with this youngest age range.
- In Wales, the main focus of development is on the Foundation Phase for young children from three to seven years, bridging the early years curriculum into the first years of primary school. There is no national under threes guidance in Wales.
- In Northern Ireland the early years curriculum applies to three- and four-year-olds, often mainly threes. There is no national under threes guidance and the main focus for current development has been the Foundation Stage that applies to the first two years of primary school, with children aged four or five years of age. However, over 2009 the Department of Education is working on an early years strategy for the age span of birth to six years.

The English and Scottish under threes materials had a different appearance and overall structure, but otherwise they had a great deal in common, because the teams drew on the same source materials, including research about very early development. These strands for good practice now run throughout the 0-5 EYFS as consistent themes in developmentally appropriate practice: the importance of secure attachment within early childhood, that making a personal relationship with children is a non-negotiable part of early years professionalism and that nurture is an essential part of good and safe practice.

Development matters in the Early Years Foundation Stage (EYFS)

All early years practitioners in England need to have become familiar with the details of the EYFS but the good practice described is not new. Part of your task, in finding your way around the EYFS materials, is to recognise just how much is familiar when your early years provision already has good practice. (See page 61 for information on how to access materials about the EYFS.) There has been an adjustment for those practitioners who were at ease with the structure of the Birth to Three framework. The EYFS follows the six areas of learning and development pattern that was established from 2000 in the Foundation Stage for over threes. However, considerable amounts of the Birth to Three Matters materials have been incorporated in the EYFS.

There are six areas of learning and development within the EYFS.

- Personal, social and emotional development
- Communication, language and literacy
- Problem solving, reasoning and numeracy
- Knowledge and understanding of the world
- Physical development
- Creative development

This framework is one way of considering the breadth of children's learning. But of course children do not learn in separate compartments; the whole point is that children's learning crosses all the boundaries. The aim of identifying areas of learning is to help adults to create a balance, to address all the different, equally important areas of what children gain across the years of early childhood.

Now that the EYFS is in place, children's personal records and any other materials, such as displays, that show their learning in action, need to be connected, in a meaningful way, with the six areas of learning. A detailed resource of developmental information and practical advice is provided in the Practice Guidance booklet of the EYFS, in Appendix 2 that runs from pages 24-116. None of this material should be used as have-to-do grids. It is crucial that early years practitioners and teams hold tight to this key point, and it is stated clearly in paragraph 2.1, page 11 of the *Practice Guidance*.

'Each section of the areas of Learning and Development offers examples of the types of activities and experiences that children might be involved in as they progress and which practitioners could refer to when they are planning. There is also support for continuous assessment that practitioners must undertake. These sections are not intended to be exhaustive – different children will do things at different times - and they should not be used as checklists.'

In each of these very full pages, the same pattern applies.

- The developmental information in the first column, Development matters, is a reminder of the kinds of changes likely to happen – not the final list of what happens, and in this exact way. The examples work like the Development Matters box on each of the Birth to Three cards or the Stepping Stones in the Foundation Stage.

- The broad and overlapping age spans are deliberate: birth to 11 months, 8-20 months, 16-26 months, 22-36 months, 30-50 months and 40-60+ months. The aim is to refresh about development, supporting practitioners to take time over all the 'steps'. There should be no headlong rush to the 'older' age spans, let alone the final early learning goals (ELGs). None of the descriptions, apart from the ELGs, are required targets or outcomes. They are aimed at enabling practitioners to focus on the nature and interests of younger children.
- So, the only part of all this information that is statutory is the description of the early learning goals. They only become relevant for direct observation within the last year of the EYFS (just like with the Foundation Stage), which is the reception class located in primary schools.
- Practitioners working with babies should look at the birth to 11 months and the 8-20 months spans. If you spend time with toddlers, then the 8-20 months and the 16-26 months are appropriate reminders.
- If you work with babies or toddlers whose development is already being slowed by disability or very limited early experience, then of course look at an appropriate younger band. You can only identify appropriate next steps from a baby's or toddler's current point of development.

A learning journey from day one

The ELGs placed at the end of every 40-60+ age band cannot be used to shape the experiences of ones and nearly twos in any meaningful way. The whole point about the developmental information in the earlier age bands of these pages of the Practice Guidance is to bring alive what those events – way into the future – look like for babies and toddlers.

The learning journey of early childhood starts with babies – in fact research into brain development prior to birth tells us that even newborns have already been learning in the womb. Infants are poised to go; they are not a blank slate. However, the misleading message is often that 'babies are boring' or 'they don't do anything' or 'they don't start learning until...' It is crucial that practitioners working with babies and young toddlers are alert to very early learning. For instance, that babies develop essential communication skills long before the first recognisable words, or that they have growing knowledge and understanding of their own world.

Child-focussed observation and planning

It has been necessary for practitioners (in England) to adjust their flexible forward planning and child-focussed documentation to reflect these six areas and to leave behind the aspects and components structure of Birth to Three Matters. However, the six areas should not be daunting, since early years practitioners should have a sound basis of child development knowledge. If any practitioners feel unsure of realistic expectations, then the *Development Matters* column can be used as one way to refresh that knowledge.

The situation about any kind of written planning and documentation is the same as has applied all the time for Birth to Three and the Foundation Stage, namely that there are no statutory written formats for observation and planning. The early years inspection body for England, Ofsted, does not require any specific approach to the need to be observant and to have a planful approach. The EYFS materials offer suggestions, including the flexible approach of the Learning Journey, which is described on the CD-ROM materials linked with the Principles into Practice card 3.1 *Observation, assessment and planning*. But no format is compulsory.

Being a helpful adult

The Development Matters column was not designed as a profile for developmental tracking. It is not required – within the statutory guidance - that practitioners collect evidence against all, or even a large selection, of these items. If any readers have been told that they should record in that way, then be aware that this direction is not part of the EYFS national, statutory requirements. It has been a local decision or is the particular stance of a given trainer or organisation that has produced assessment materials.

The descriptions are precisely that – examples of some of the changes to which practitioners should be alert. They are not statutory goals or outcomes, necessary developmental milestones or, in the snappy media phrase, government-required 'targets for toddlers'.

There is also a fair amount of repetition, or near-repetition, across the strands in the six areas of learning and development. This overlap further shows that the Development Matters columns were not designed as a tracking instrument, but also confirms that, of course, a recognisable skill or outlook from a baby or child supports more than one aspect of early learning. They do not learn in separate categories.

The materials for the EYFS also confirm what has always been the situation for Birth to Three Matters and for the Foundation Stage: flexible planning through topics is one way of looking ahead, but the method is not compulsory. Additionally, briefing papers, for instance again on the CD-ROM against card 3.1 confirm that topic based planning is not suitable for younger children, the under threes. Run very flexibly, a topic may respond to the interests of the rising threes. But it does not fit the knowledge base and ways of learning for toddlers and babies.

The key messages from the EYFS materials are that any formats used by practitioners need to show:

- The progress of individual children over time, at their own pace and set against realistic expectations for their age, ability and experiences.
- That planning is responsive to the needs and interests of individual children: through continuous provision (the learning environment) and flexible use of adult-planned activities.
- How observations of children make a difference to what is offered to individuals and to sensible short-term changes to special experiences made available to any of the babies or toddlers.
- There is plenty of scope for fine-tuning through short-term planning – that 'what next?' or 'next steps' are a real part of the process.

Over the pages 24-116, the EYFS Practice Guidance has other information and suggestions:

- *Look, listen and note* (second column in from the left) is a resource of suggestions, very like the box with the same title that appeared on each of the Birth to Three cards and the 'Examples of what children do' in the Foundation Stage. Again this is not a list of the observations everyone has to do; they are reminders of the pitch and level at which it makes sense to observe across that age range.
- The other two columns - *Effective practice* and *Planning and resourcing* - are like the boxes on the Birth to Three cards and the right hand pages throughout the Foundation Stage file entitled 'What does the practitioner need to do?' They are ideas: some of which you may already do, and some will give you a fresh look. You may not agree with all the suggestions, or with the age band in which they are placed. I certainly challenge a few of the suggestions as inappropriate for the understanding of the younger age groups.

How to be a helpful adult to babies and young toddlers

It is complicated to explain and predict how young children manage some of their impressive developmental achievements. For instance, no single theory can fully explain how toddlers learn to speak a language within the very early years, with some toddlers learning more than one language. But the consistent messages about how we can help do not point to complex techniques.

The best interactions, experiences and opportunities for babies and toddlers are straightforward. What benefits young learning is simple, for instance see the section about communication on page 00. Some practitioners may also dismiss the simpler ideas as 'just common sense'. But what seems obvious to some practitioners, as the right way to behave with very young children, may not seem at all a clear choice to another practitioner, or to a parent (or vice versa).

Sometimes the puzzle that needs to be solved is why practitioners, or parents, discount simple approaches and play resources. Some difficulties arise because uncertain practitioners try to organise a day for babies and very young children that depends on their tolerating group activities.

Under ones and toddlers operate as individuals, and even more than twos, threes and fours, are deeply unimpressed by having to sit 'nicely' or wait for their turn – whether that is to communicate with a familiar adult or to get their hands on an interesting resource. In the end, developmentally appropriate practice with the under ones and toddlers has a great deal in common with good practice across early childhood, as the following sections will describe and explain.

Personal, Social and Emotional Development

The *Birth to Three Matters* framework (for England) and *Birth to Three* (for Scotland) both placed a strong emphasis on the importance of secure attachment and of close, affectionate relationships for young children. Both documents took the line that good quality in group care was not possible without a proper key person system. The 0-5 Early Years Foundation Stage (for England) has taken that essential good practice guidance and applied it across early childhood. This section focuses especially on babies and young toddlers, but these crucial PSED points do not fade away as the months and years pass.

Care and a nurturing environment

Ones, like any of the youngest children in the 0-5 years span, have historically been classified as in 'care' facilities, in contrast with 'early educational' settings. The care/education division always was an artificial and nonsensical split, when viewed from the perspective of young children. Care – or nurture - and early learning are inseparable, and good early years practice in any kind of provision is always organised around that central understanding.

Unfortunately, official statements and the structure of much inspection have persisted in presenting the two as separate. This approach would matter less if it were separate yet equal, but care and caring are so often treated as the poor relation. If adults undervalue care, that attitude has a negative effect on the quality of provision for three- to five-year-olds. However, a disrespectful 'only care' outlook has really serious consequences for babies and toddlers, because they need demonstrably more caring support for their physical needs. If the personal times of changing, feeding, resting, dressing and undressing are seen as 'wasted' time, then a significant proportion of every day with this very young age group is dismissed as time when 'nothing important happens'.

The avowed aim of the EYFS has been to establish a coherent early childhood framework in which the care-education division is bridged and removed. Whether the artificial distinction really does disappear will depend upon continued effort to deal with a history of different qualifications, professional status and a persistent outlook that time spent with children only becomes more valuable the closer they are to the age of statutory education. It will not be much of an achievement – for babies and young children - if the only change with the EYFS is to merge two inspections into one. You can read more about care of physical needs later in this section, in the context of the key person system and also on page 49 within 'Self care', part of the chapter on Physical Development.

The social world of babies

Most babies are born sociable; they are motivated to make connections with those adults who will become familiar. Babies use eye contact, sometimes a piercing and steady stare, and sound making, including crying, along with touch and a quite tight hold around manageable bits of the human body, such as fingers or hair. Alert adults notice if young babies show few signs of being social, although in the early weeks and months it can be hard to assess what is wrong. Babies show a unique temperament from the earliest weeks, and some babies are noticeably more vocal and physically lively from the outset.

Food for thought

Friendly, affectionate touch and easy physical contact is part of every day life for babies and young toddlers. Babies show that they like to be close – not to any random adult, but with easy snuggling access to their familiar adults in the family and out-of-home care.

Of course, babies - no more than toddlers or young children - should have cuddles foisted upon them, because the adult wants the contact. Considerate adults are easily available for babies and are sensitive to this baby's current mood and how they like, in general, to be touched and handled. This sensitivity creates the template for later interactions. Certainly, adults should not withdraw from comfortable physical contact and human touch, because babies have become children.

Some practitioners, and teams, have become highly anxious about touch, and consequently risk losing focus on the welfare of babies and very young children. There is nothing in the EYFS Welfare Requirements (in the Statutory Guidance) about restricting physical contact with any young children. Nor is there any national requirement about always having two practitioners present, for instance as part of witnessing procedures for personal care.

For babies and toddlers, the personal, social and emotional are all intertwined:

- They discover themselves, including the boundaries to their own body. But they need close physical contact and affectionate communication that gives them a sense of other people: their parents and a small number of other familiar adults, as well as their siblings.
- Their social life depends on the security of familiar routines, faces and ways of being handled. Even the most 'come-what-may' babies want some predictability in their life, so they can learn what is usual, and make sense of what is less usual or surprising.
- Their emotional life depends on feeling safe: that their physical needs will be met, that crying brings a familiar face and that familiar person will sooth their discomfort, as well as make the most of their increasing wakefulness for chat and play.

Some babies and young toddlers will spend those early months within their own family, although it is very unlikely that they will only spend time with their parents. Unless a family, or lone parent, is very isolated (a reason for concern and offering support), the social world of babies includes some time with their extended family and family friends. Some babies will start out-of-home care within the first year: with a childminder or in the baby room of a group setting. Babies can cope with more than one familiar adult but they cannot manage the changes if there are too many faces, bodies, smells and styles of care. So it is crucial, a non-negotiable part of good and safe practice, that group provision is deliberately organised in ways that ensure babies and young children can form an emotional attachment to one or two practitioners.

A home-like atmosphere

The EYFS is very clear about the kind of environment that should be created across all provision for early childhood. The following sentences are a crucial message: 'The EYFS sets standards to enable early years providers to reflect the rich and personalised experience that many parents give their children at home. Like parents, providers should deliver individualised learning, development and care that enhances the development of the children in their care and gives those children the best possible start in life.' (*Statutory Framework*, page 9, paragraph 1.13)

The PSED area of learning and development comes alive when practitioners value nurturing babies and very young children.

A non-negotiable part of good practice is that a key person system is established in all group provision. Childminders are, by practical definition, the children's key person. This practice is now statutory for the EYFS and is described in the Welfare Requirements (page 37 in the *Statutory Framework*). The personal and emotional development of babies is supported, when they have continuing experience of a familiar person, who – like their parents – has become more and more able to recognise this baby's mood and the different reasons that probably underlie those emotions.

- Good quality practice means that babies receive prompt attention when the signs are that they are hungry, thirsty or need their nappy changed.
- A supportive key person has learned, with the help of parents, how this baby shows tiredness and is ready for a daytime sleep.
- However, sensitive early years practitioners do not assume that fretfulness or complaining sounds are always signs that an older baby or toddler needs to be settled for sleep. Sometimes restlessness or physical fidgeting is a sign that this baby wants attention, movement, a trip out or something interesting to be shared with him or her.
- Babies are helped by friendly, yet flexible routines and adult patience as they move slowly towards a daily routine that is more 'convenient' for adults.

Being a helpful adult

Part of a close and personal relationship with babies and toddlers is that you are a welcome and playful companion: close, looking interested, responding and following the flow of the baby or young toddler's interests right now. Even good quality play resources will not do the job on their own, what adults do is the crucial component. The entire toy industry cannot come up with anything for babies and toddlers that can replace a kindly, playful, familiar adult.

Some bought play resources are very useful – the more open-ended materials that give plenty of scope for baby choice and exploration. However, some manufactured toys are a waste of space and money.

We live in a technological age, but babies do not need or benefit from technological toys, nor from an environment dominated by primary colours, plastic and background noise from battery-operated toys that will not shut up. Twenty-first century babies and toddlers are still keen on the potential of cardboard boxes, saucepans and wooden spoons.

For example

It is possible for the key person to take responsibility for most of the personal care of their key babies or toddlers. I have observed this pattern working smoothly in nurseries, where the team and the manager are committed to the emotional well being of babies. This personal way of organising often goes hand in hand with the full recognition that babies and toddlers deserve the respect of a personal routine. They are changed when they need their nappy changed and not as part of an 'every baby gets changed' convenience routine.

- In Southlands Crèche, the key person undertakes the nappy changing and feeding. Toddlers, who have shown the awareness that they are ready for toilet training, are taken by their key person at regular times that are attuned to this child. There are daily conversations between the key person and parent, as they share the daily record and highlights of a baby or toddler's day.
- In Grove House Infant and Toddler Centre, the key person undertakes their key children's personal care. The centre has the built-in nappy changing area with an integral set of steps that can be pulled out. This facility means that, once toddlers are steady on their feet, they can be active in this routine by climbing up the steps and, with help, positioning themselves on the comfortable changing area. Everything that is needed, including individual toiletry baskets, is within adult reaching distance.

The section of the EYFS quoted earlier emphasises the non-negotiable part that 'care' plays in acceptable provision and applies across the age range 0 - 5. So the kind of homely practice that should be established for babies and toddlers, wherever they spend their days, is the youngest version of the home-like atmosphere that should be visible right up to and including reception class. Even those five-year-olds are to be treated as young children, enjoying the final year of their early years provision; they are not to be treated as little school pupils.

Childminders may seem to have a head start when it comes to opportunities for a family atmosphere and personal relationships developing within an actual home. Yet, the best of group provision has always rested on a homely physical environment and emotional atmosphere. The messages of the EYFS – what is actually said in the pack and not the misrepresentations – are very clear that childminders should be encouraged to continue to operate in this home-like way. They are certainly not required them to turn their homes into a structured and inappropriate classroom model.

Very personal interaction

In time, children come to feel part of a slightly larger community. But the perspective of a baby or toddler is that of a family group – may be an extended family, but a very small community none the less. When you are responsible for ones, you need that you keep this understanding to the top of your mind. Babies and young toddlers (and older children still within early childhood) need to feel like individuals. They are not well served if the organisation of a group setting 'loses' their individuality within too large a group. It is a measure of a genuine community that the interests and perspectives of the youngest members are never subsumed under what works, or seems to work, for older members.

Unless you work as a childminder or in a very small nursery (or intimate baby room), you need to ensure that you have regular - ideally daily - time with your key children. Elinor Goldschmied described this close, being together time as 'the island of intimacy'. It is a protected time, especially in what may feel like a busy nursery day.

- The main point of this time is that you are together, without interruptions, with the children. What you do within this 15-20 minutes is entirely influenced by the current interests of the babies or toddlers.
- You will judge on the day whether this very little group wants to snuggle into a comfy area and enjoy a book or a song. But the island of intimacy is not exclusively a sit- or lie-down time.
- I have known key person time be the enjoyable opportunity to 'go visiting': to another section of a large centre, to say hello to the manager or the cook and to explore the 'big children's garden' since they are busy inside.

The special key group times are experiences that do not stop once children are no longer babies and toddlers. All young children need this kind of time to enjoy an individual relationship with their key person.

Babies and toddlers are individuals and they need small, intimate times. They do not 'do' groups; it is developmentally inappropriate to attempt anything larger than what I call a sofa-full. It is a different matter if several babies or toddlers enthusiastically move across to get fully engaged in interesting resources. Alternatively, you may find yourself surrounded by a number of bobbing

Food for thought

The Scottish Birth to Three guidance included the key idea that young children need to feel 'kept in mind'. This concept does not only apply to babies or other under threes; it is crucial across the age range.

Young children need to feel that that can feel secure in the safety and comfort of your arms and lap. They need to be held and to hold in their turn. However, even babies need to feel that emotional foundation that they have a secure place in your mind – your thoughts and feelings.

You might like to think about how even babies can feel that you definitely have space for them, as individuals, in your mind. Also talk with colleagues, if you work in a team or are part of a childminding network.

- You might start with how you show babies you are glad to see them, after a short gap, like the weekend.
- How do you make their personal care routines special for them – the fine tuning for baby and young toddler preference that means it definitely is not a one-size-fits-all for feeding or nappy changing.

Food for thought

When you organise and manage time with children's well being at the heart of your decisions, then you gain an understanding of what I call the 'big little things' that matter in a child's world. By this phrase I mean that what may seem minor side issues to adults can be a big new perspective for young children.

For example, I recall a nursery team who were based in part of a large building that included a leisure centre. They described to me how they had recently taken small groups of children for a walk around the centre. These children were entranced and were old enough to talk about the experience. They entered the nursery through a side door and had no idea that all these interesting sights, many of which could be watched from the upper gallery of the centre, were part of the same building.

The nursery team was immediately responsive to the personal views of the children, recognised that the stroll had opened up new vistas for knowledge and understanding of the world of these three- and four-year-olds. The team was definitely going to continue this internal visit on a regular basis.

young toddlers who have chosen to join what started as one adult dancing around with a baby in her or his arms. These are spontaneous and physically active events that evolve because babies and toddlers have made that choice.

Some readers may have been given the advice or direction that they should plan group activities and expect babies and toddlers to join. I have encountered advice that circle time should be extended to the babies, with the argument that this experience will help them in the transition to an older room, where this event will be part of a normal day.

- I disagree with this advice – firstly for the developmental reasons outlined. Even if the plan is that babies experience singing, it is still much better practice to offer songs and rhymes in an informal way, as and when babies would like this, or when toddlers indicate that they want a familiar song.
- It is also important to challenge any approach to transition that rests upon importing practice with older children into a younger age range. *Good practice with transition is to establish continuity through taking what works well with the younger age range into the next room or next setting.*

Being a helpful adult

- You can guide older babies and toddlers towards kindly behaviour but you need to keep your adult language very simple indeed. Recall that babies and very young children are physical; they do not have the understanding to be 'aggressive'.
- However, physically rough strategies – perhaps to secure a toy they want - need to be converted, with your direct guidance, towards other options. You move in calmly, ideally before babies or toddlers have become tearful and ensure that everyone is safe.
- You acknowledge with words that, 'You both want the teddy' and, depending on your knowledge of these individuals, you may gather both babies and the teddy into your lap. You may discretely pull in another soft toy that you guess could be equally attractive.

A learning journey towards self regulation

The EYFS places a strong emphasis on sound knowledge of child development; that early years practitioners have to rest their reactions and forward thinking on realistic expectations for the age group. This direction is central for any kind of sensible approach to the behaviour of babies and toddlers. They are at the very beginning of a learning journey to establish habits of positive, prosocial behaviour and to learn to guide themselves and exercise self control.

Babies have neither the understanding, nor the plotting power, to be held accountable for the consequences of their actions. Babies cry – it is their main form of communication in the early weeks, and some babies cry a very great deal. Undoubtedly, it is emotionally exhausting when you care for a baby who is hard to comfort. But they are not setting out to destroy your wellbeing. The only way sometimes is to accept that you will hold him or her a great deal – and in a group setting it will be the baby's key person who takes this responsibility. Touch, hold, rocking and cuddling will be a crucial part of reassuring the baby, as well as calm talking or singing.

- You remain alert to what may be the main explanation for the crying. Sometimes there is a physical reason, but sometimes it is emotional. Occasionally, an older baby or young toddler is effectively crying out, 'Nothing personal, but I really don't want to be here.'
- Sometimes you simply do not know why this baby continues to be harder to comfort than another of a similar age. If your relationship stretches into the future, then this 'cross' baby may grow into a firm toddler and two-year-old. At that point, she or he may find daily life much more straightforward, now that preferences and objections can be expressed in spoken words.

Food for thought

As with any other aspect of early development, the behaviour elements in the PSED strand have to be grounded in realistic expectations. The learning journey towards self regulation is a long one and progresses step by step. Young children are helped by patient adults, who expect enough but not too much and who are ready to say, and do, the same thing again and again.

At 12 months, my daughter Tanith showed every sign that she understood basic house rules like, 'not the plants' and 'not the video'. We did not have many of these 'not' rules, since most items had never come down from upper shelves, where they were placed when her brother was born two years earlier.

But it was something of a game to Tanith to go close to the video player, move a hand towards the opening and then turn to look back meaningfully at us. The message of body language seemed unmistakably to be, 'Will you stop me?' It was crucial that we did confirm a friendly but firm 'no', followed up by moving her away and into something interesting.

Young children do not have the understanding to 'plot' against their familiar adults. But by the end of the baby year, they are able to test you in this way. Have you encountered this almost teasing behaviour from very young toddlers?

- It is crucial that early practitioners are not harsh on themselves with judgments like, 'Why can't I stop her crying?' Equally, if you work with colleagues in a group setting, there must be full team support for the focus of a key person, whose key baby is distraught. It is never spoiling to calm and cuddle a distressed baby or young child.
- In the happiest of families there will be times of uncertainty or trouble. Babies and very young children sense their parents' unease and may express that through their behaviour during their time with you. You need to offer comfort and patience to the baby or toddler and a friendly comment/question to parents that gives them the opportunity to comment on your observation that 'Tyra hasn't seemed her usual self this week.'

Babies and very young toddlers experience strong emotions, but they express themselves through actions and their body language. They are as yet unable to put those feelings into words. You help them on this particular learning journey by offering empathy with very young children. You get to know them as individuals, so you are more able to make a good guess about how they probably feel. You use your own emotional vocabulary, long before you would expect a baby or young toddler to understand or use words that describe emotion. You set the scene for learning, because your words, backed up by your body language, communicate, 'You look happy. What a wonderful, big smile!' or 'You sound upset. Let's see what we can do to make things better.'

For example

Babies and young toddlers make social moves towards each other and regular contact within their early years provision creates the recognition that is the basis for very young friendships. During my time with the under threes team of Grove House Children's Centre, I was able to observe how the practitioners were close to the babies and toddlers. So they were able to support young social interaction and help out if necessary.

- Babies and toddlers were often interested in each other. Indoors, there was always a practitioner sitting close to children, often on the floor with them. So, it was straightforward to guide gently, if young attempts to make contact by touch were a bit too vigorous for the other baby or toddler. I observed more than one occasion when a practitioner patiently helped one older toddler or two-year-old to say to another, 'I don't like it. Don't.'
- Like any normal day with very young children, the adults themselves were sometimes on the receiving end of friendly pats that became slightly more forceful. Again, children were gently guided by words and a facial expression that communicated, 'That's not how we treat friends.'

Babies and young toddlers do not understand the concept of 'sharing' and they are not able to wait for 'their turn'.

- The Grove House team helped by continuing to develop a learning environment with generous resources, organised in baskets, which toddlers were able to pull out for themselves.
- Because practitioners were on the floor with the children, they were able to ensure that resources were within reach and discreetly to move across items if one baby or toddler had only a few.
- Consequently, actual turn taking and waiting did not arise too often. When the group was outdoors sometimes it could become an issue if several children all wanted to use the wheeled vehicles. Adults were then able to negotiate with the young children and find a way, without this kind of discussion having to happen a very great deal throughout the day.

It is not developmentally appropriate to label babies or toddlers as 'clingy', or treat that pattern of behaviour as a 'problem'. It is very normal that this age group wants to be close to a familiar adult – that is why you will sometimes be in a cuddle-huddle with several babies or toddlers. Babies and toddlers will head away from you, their key person, when they feel secure. They will hold tight or want to be very close when they do not feel okay, or are uncertain for some reason. They will show you when they are comfortable to extend the invisible elastic and move away, although they may well check on you by looking. It is inevitable within shared care that the adults – parents and practitioners – need to ease the handover at the beginning and end of the day.

- You help a baby or toddler with the daily separation from their parent when you are ready to reassure, cuddle and talk gently. The baby, as well as parent, needs to feel that there is an unrushed transfer from one safe pair of hands over to another.
- A key person should have become familiar with this baby or young toddler, so you do not opt for distraction with random toys. You have learned that this young child is reassured by staring together at a particular picture or going into the garden. Your response is based on your knowledge and personal relationship.

Communication, Language and Literacy

Food for thought

Children need good reasons – from their point of view – to want to talk and to listen. They need plenty of early experiences of familiar adults who listen to them. Normal life for toddlers and young children is having to struggle with the search for words and tolerating the frustrations of making other people understand.

Babies and toddlers will persevere in this task and will relish personal exchanges when their key person, parent and other familiar adults show that they genuinely enjoy chatting with this older baby and toddler right now. Young toddlers forgive those times when a familiar adult seems to be very dense and fails to understand what is obvious to the gesticulating toddler.

The Every Child a Talker (ECaT) programme, launched by the Department for Children Schools and Families in 2009, addresses the need for everyone to focus on communication over early childhood. The guidance homes in on the serious consequences for children when their early experiences have not supported them to become communicative, keen to talk and voice their ideas, able to listen and to participate in the turn taking of genuine conversation.

There can be a significant gap in the size of children's working vocabulary between those who have had a good start in communication and those children who have been poorly served by their early experiences.

- The desire to communicate and the steady building of vocabulary are well supported by natural, daily exchanges that arise through shared play and joint experiences.
- Helpful adults do not sit down to plan structured 'communication activities' – not with any young children and certainly not with babies or toddlers.
- Communication is personal and flows from what interests this baby, toddler or child today. Simple works - what really matters is that adults listen to, talk with, interact and play with babies and young children.
- The support from a planful adult outlook is that opportunities and experiences are offered (not imposed) which, from practitioners' knowledge of individual children, are likely to interest and excite them.
- Young children will not need special language programmes and remedial help, so long as their early years have been full of personal, attentive communication – at home but also in their out-of-home provision.

Babies as active communicators

Observant parents and early years practitioners have always commented on the alertness of babies and how much happens before the first recognisable words. Mothers, and involved fathers too, were sure that their babies were responding with interest to what was said, long before they could understand any of the content expressed in words. The options from video technology in the 1970s led to very detailed research projects in which babies of only a few months old and their mothers were filmed in close interaction. The video footage was then analysed frame by frame. Several research teams were active in this work and one was led by Colwyn Trevarthen, who is still fully engaged in research about the patterns of very early communication

It became clear that:

- Young babies were an active partner in these very early conversations and not simply passive followers of what their mother did. They imitated their mother's expression but were also active in their own facial expressions and waving hands and feet.

- Babies were able to pause and look expectant. They had learned something of the timing of a conversation, because their mother communicated regularly in this way.
- Babies reacted to changes in their mother's tone. They were also very aware if their mother's attention was distracted, as was sometimes deliberately created by an interruption in some studies. Babies made physically active and sound-making attempts to regain her full attention.
- There was also evidence that the babies had a subtle grasp of the give-and-take of a proper exchange. When babies were shown a video of their mother, they soon changed from happy communication to signs of confusion, and then distress. The only interpretation was that the reactions of the familiar face on the screen failed to fit what the baby had just 'said'. The timing was awry, the video of the mother's reactions were not attuned to the emotional tone of her real baby. Young babies very soon became aware of the mismatch.

The 1970s and 1980s studies used mother and baby pairs and called the subtle adult communication with babies 'motherese'. However, this kind of adjusted communication, that is so very suitable for babies, is not the sole territory of mothers, nor of women. Nor is the communication style used only by parents, so 'parentese' is not much of an improvement as a term. Men, as fathers or early years practitioners, are completely capable of adjusting their communication in this way. So it is better called a phrase like 'infant-directed speech'. Older children, who probably copy familiar adults, also sometimes produce this kind of talk with babies they know, not always their own siblings. The delighted reaction from the baby is encouragement to continue.

The characteristics of effective infant-directed speech are as follows:

- You have to be close to babies so that your faces are in close proximity and they can see your eyes and facial expression. You might be chatting in this way as you change their nappy, sitting with them on your lap or beside them as they lay on their back on a comfortable floor.
- It does not matter what you say, so long as you look interested. Use ordinary words, there is no advantage, and some drawbacks, if you introduce 'baby talk' and change words, like saying 'bikky' or 'gee gee'.
- Keep what you say simple and your phrases short. Pause and look expectant, so that the baby learns it is now her turn to 'say' something.
- Be more expressive than in usual speech, both in how you say the words and in your facial expressions. Use your eyes, mouth and facial muscles to add to the communication.
- Babies seem to like voices to be slightly higher pitched than the normal adult tone. On average, women have a higher pitched voice, but men can go up a bit in pitch without straining or sounding odd. For instance, watch three-month old Charlotte and her father, as he changes her nappy and chats, in *Firm foundations for early literacy* (Siren Films 2009).
- What works best is sing-song style, with a circling and repetitive quality. You repeat or half-repeat a phrase that has caught the baby's attention, such as, 'Is that a raspberry? Did you blow a raspberry at me?'
- Follow a relaxed rhythm, so the baby has the time to express their sounds, make their facial expression or wave their hands at you. If you go too fast, then you end up talking over the baby's contribution to the conversation.
- Be ready to follow the baby's lead, in sounds or facial expression. You are partners in this exchange and it is a delight to babies (and toddlers as well) when you copy them.

Watch out carefully for these skills in babies whom you know. You can also watch a visual record of active babies in the DVD materials listed on page 63. I was in the position to make detailed observations of the early communication skills of my daughter Tanith. Of course, the pattern is not identical for all babies, so you could consider in what kinds of ways you have noticed similar developments with very young babies, with whom you now spend your time.

For example

- Babies are individuals from the very beginning. Tanith was a rather serious baby at the outset and frowned quite a lot. Fleeting smiles seemed to be there at around six weeks – some babies have a definite smile by 4-6 weeks. But I was not certain with Tanith until closer to seven or eight weeks. Then one morning, I was chatting to her, teasing her about what a pain she was with all the night waking, and she gave me a full beaming grin.
- At seven to eight weeks she had a range of cooing sounds and soft aahs, as well as a strong cry. What appeared to be deliberate gurgling noises soon followed.
- Over her third month, Tanith's ability to stare at people's faces really seemed to be a strategy to communicate. Her face lit up at a response and she usually made a stream of sounds, kicked her legs and moved her arms about in a lively fashion.
- In her fourth month, Tanith held sustained 'conversations' with us and sometimes laughed with her mouth wide open. Her sound making and turn- taking in communication extended over the weeks.
- Over 6-7 months Tanith's communication included double-syllable sounds and long strings of sound in a sustained flow. She had also started to lean in towards us as she 'spoke'.
- By her ninth month, she definitely turned in a reliable way in repsonse to her name, whether we used it or Drew - her brother who was two years older and liked to get his baby sister's personal attention in this way. Tanith liked to have Drew play with her, and rewarded him with big smiles. One of her favourites was playing 'nose', which was basically a game of touching nose-to-nose.
- Towards the end of her baby year, Tanith's own utterances had become very chatty, her pattern of sounds had conversational expression and pacing. She could definitely hold her own in a turn-taking conversation, in which her contribution did not include any recognisable words as yet.

For example

One exciting part of tracking toddlers' language development is realising how closely the first words connect with what is familiar to and makes sense to this very young girl or boy.

- At 13 months Tanith had the beginnings of what sounded like attempts at words and over 14-15 months I noted down what I felt were definitely words. In between these early words, Tanith filled the gaps – like any toddler – with a great deal of highly expressive word-like jargon and gesturing.
- Tanith's first recognisable words arose from authentic experiences within her daily life and her familiar and regular routines. For instance, she had 'ca' applied to the family cat and increasingly to other cats she could see in the neighbourhood when we went out and about locally. Tanith also used 'bubbles' – reflecting her daily experience of a lot of blowing bubbles, playing with foamy water and baby bubble bath at night.
- By 18 months she used words for familiar items: shoe, stick, car, mil(k), chee(se), ca(t), train (which came out more like 'dee'), dog, sock, gop (her vitamin drops), coco (pops), chip, bin, bag, key and book. She also had a range of useful words that would operate as requests, descriptions or suggestions: all gone, no more, down, up, go and look.

Tracking toddlers' early, recognisable words can be an absorbing joint project with their parent(s). Detailed, written reports of early development remind you how much spoken language is dependent on experiences.

- Annette Karmiloff-Smith (1994) describes the development of the children who were part of the 'Baby it's you' project, and you can watch the children in the DVD. One child has 'peas' as one of his early words, but he likes eating this food. Another toddler who enjoys jigsaw puzzles is motivated to have a go at that word, although it emerges more like 'puggall'.
- Robin Campbell (1999) documented the first five years of his granddaughter, Alice. His description highlights how some of Alice's early spoken words were directly connected with her favourite books, which she had heard out of choice many times. You may notice how toddlers, with whom you are familiar, are able to direct you to a favourite book by key words and to join in an active way.
- Young children enjoy songs and rhymes and some of those early words are a very personal version of part of a song. I am regularly struck by how easily toddlers in a day nursery learn key words from familiar nursery rhymes, as well as the hand movements.
- In order to understand some of Tanith's words, you needed to be familiar with her experience of music in the family. For instance, 'ga-ga' referred to 'Radio Ga Ga' by Queen and 'rock' was a request for 'Fraggle Rock', the theme from a popular children's programme at that time.

Puggall!

Communication with older babies and young toddlers

Older babies become very chatty because they have had generous personal attention over their early months. The principles of infant directed speech flow into good communication with older babies whose sound making can now be very active. They are also able to use gesture to indicate what is of current interest to them. They will look at something intently, point with their eyes, then point with a finger or whole hand. What works best continues to be very simple, not complicated 'communication techniques'. Firm foundations for early communication skills rest upon generous time one-to-one with babies, alongside the carefully shared attention when you have two, or at most three older babies snuggled up around you.

Key issues are:

- You have to be close to the baby or young toddler, you cannot communicate across a distance. You should be close enough to touch. You get and stay on their level and make friendly eye contact. It cannot be stressed enough that communication with babies and young children is between individuals – an adult and very few children. No sensible adult tries to do group work with babies and toddlers.
- Make sure you have their attention before you start, by using gentle touch, eye contact and a smile or the baby's name. You will notice when it is clear that their personal name has meaning. If background noise is a problem, find ways to create peacefulness
- Pause and then say something, or point out something of interest. Sometimes, the communication starts because this baby or young toddler has engaged your attention.
- A conversation needs a shared focus on what is in front of both of you. So follow the lead of babies and young toddlers. Look at where their eyes are directed, listen to what they say and comment on their contribution. Ensure that your words and simple phrases connect with what babies and toddlers experience right here.
- Look and sound interested – mobile babies and toddlers choose not to spend time with adults who are dull and hard work. You use facial expression and your tone to express your interest in this box, feeling the soft material or making funny faces.
- Avoid taking over the talk. Trust the power of the pause, that gap when the baby or young toddler will think and make their own contribution. This point continues to be central to communication with children. Avoid being in a rush to fill an uncomfortable silence. Babies and children need time to reflect and react, along with what they say – in words or sounds and gestures.
- You may sometimes repeat what a toddler says and extend a little by adding a relevant comment. For instance, an older baby or young toddler directs your attention to the big sunflowers, swaying the breeze. Perhaps she or he tries their personal word that is close to 'flower'. You respond with something like, 'Yes, look at our sunflowers', then pause and add, 'See them move from side to side', and use a gesture that mimics the swaying of the flowers.
- You say any words correctly as you reply – so a word-sound like 'fower' is reflected back as 'flower' with all the sounds that make up that word. But you do not make the toddler repeat the correct version, because this kind of pressure can be disheartening. In a relaxed atmosphere, you will often hear a toddler echo what you have said – they do their own practice.

Your communication with babies and toddlers needs to be adjusted to their personal temperament and their current mood. Helpful adults are not all-singing-all-dancing every moment of the day, or even over the whole session lasting a couple of hours. You, and the baby or toddler, would be exhausted. But also good communication has quieter moments: the light and shade of personal exchanges.

Two or more languages

Many children within the UK learn two or more languages over early childhood. Over time children need to be confident and competent in English, because this language is the shared language of our country and the medium of instruction in the educational system. Early years practitioners can, and should show, respect for the family language(s) as well as being responsible to help all young children become two- or five-year-olds fluent in English.

Some babies and toddlers become aware of two (or occasionally more) languages over their first or second year of life.

- It is ideal if their childminder or key person in nursery is fluent in the baby's or toddler's home language. In Grove House, this option was sometimes possible, because several of the staff team were bilingual. But frequently – given the wide diversity of languages now in the UK - this pairing will not be a possibility in a nursery.
- However, even a bilingual practitioner needs to support a toddler to build vocabulary in the language that is common to this nursery, or your home as a childminder. If you do not make this steady shift, then later this baby or toddler will not be able to talk with their two- or three-year-old peers.
- If you have no experience of the family's language, it is still possible, and friendly towards the parents and child, to learn some key phrases – perhaps of welcome and goodbye.
- But do not limit your communication with a baby or toddler to a family language in which you have a very limited vocabulary. You will restrict what the child can talk about and understand from you.
- Ask parents to help you with tapes of songs or rhymes in their home language. Or ensure that you learn a song thoroughly because this mother or father is happy to join you a few times in singing with the children.
- As with any young child, you need to find out about a young toddler's personal words, for important routines like meals, naps or nappy changing.
- The same principles of effective communication apply for very young children on the road to becoming bilingual as for monolingual children. You talk simply about what is front of both of you and the immediate experience – either in terms of this personal care routine or the open-ended resources that you are both enjoying at the moment.

The power of non-verbal communication

Adult alertness to gesture and body language is a crucial part of communication. with babies and toddlers. It will be some time before they can tell you reliably in words what they want, think and feel or what the problem is from their perspective.

Adults who spend time with babies and toddlers need to be at ease with a very expressive form of non-verbal communication and be aware of the messages of body language. There is less clear evidence, and professional disagreement, over whether practitioners and parents should use specific signs, such as those taught in the many baby signing workshops that are now available. The signs are taken from systems used for children who have serious hearing loss or another disability that affects speaking and listening. The official stance of the speech and language profession is that there is no advantage to adopting a system of signing for babies who do not have special needs related to communication.

My professional approach is to encourage what I call generosity of gesture:

- You need to be comfortable, from the early baby months, to gesture appropriately, as well as talk with babies. It often feels natural to adults to make a drinking movement

Food for thought

Sally Goddard Blythe makes strong practical points about linking communication with actual body movements. She talks about a vocabulary of the body – a rich communication which parents and practitioners need to notice and which of course never stops.

Good attention from adults to babies and toddlers is as much about looking at them as your skills of listening. Sally Goddard Blythe points out that babies show a clear response to sounds. You can tell that they are listening, because they temporarily still their physical movements. They show excitement and interest by increased physical activity, often by waving around their arms and legs.

Watch out in your own practice with babies for how their lively vocal expression by enthusiastic sound making is often preceded by an increase in motor activity. You can also observe this pattern in sequences shown in the range of DVDs listed on page 63, for instance in *The Wonder Year* from Siren Films, which documents Orson's first year of life.

Being a helpful adult

There is now a large number of commercial toys, marketed for the baby and toddler years, which are plastered with single letters and claimed to be supportive of very early learning.

However, these babies and toddler are still busy working out that people and familiar objects have names, which can be said out loud. The symbolic nature of letters – and the numbers which are often also on these plastic or soft toys – means nothing at all to them. Unfortunately, if adults have very limited understanding of the learning journey towards literacy, it may seem a good choice to buy such toys.

Early years practitioners have a professional responsibility to keep their knowledge of child development well refreshed. It is crucial that parents are not given misleading messages through the resources they see in your home as a childminder or your nursery. Likewise, you need to think always of the message given by what you fix to the walls. You provide a distorted view of the learning journey towards literacy if letter friezes dominate in a room for babies or toddlers. The same point applies if your provision is for slightly older children, whose disabilities mean their development is at a younger stage.

or put fingers to mouth when they are asking, 'Would you like a drink?' or 'Are you hungry?'
- It is crucial that gestures, just as much as actual signs (if you choose to take that route) always accompany suitable words. At no point should signing be used instead of spoken language with babies and toddlers.
- Always be close to the baby or toddler, so they can see what you are doing and you can fully notice the gesture that they make. Follow the baby or toddler's lead and copy their meaningful gestures.
- The power of some of the baby signing workshops seems to be that early years practitioners or parents are given 'permission' to get physically very close to babies and toddlers. The impact is possibly as much about emotional commitment and building a personal relationship as the actual signs.
- Ensure that you and individual babies are focussed on the same thing: follow their gaze or hold them so they can home in on your focus of attention.
- Be ready to use pointing and touch: to track a moving object, to direct a baby's attention or to emphasis a game or song, such as touching toes as part of 'where's your toes?'
- Pointing whilst used with words is a practical way to help babies and toddlers to make sense of naming words, such as 'there's your rabbit' or finding something in this page of a favourite book.
- Notice how older babies and toddlers use regular gestures to accompany their meaningful sounds and the early words, and that they do not stop gesturing once the recognisable words emerge.
- Your generous use of gesture and pointing is also a help to very young children whose home language is not that of their nursery or childminder.

The crucial point about the emphasis on positive and personal relationships in the EYFS is that shared experiences means that you get to recognise what a baby or young toddler is telling you by their actions.

- You become familiar with the combination of gestures and overall body language that this baby or toddler tends to use in order to communicate messages like, 'I'm pleased to see you', 'Who on earth is that?', 'Where's that gone?', 'Well I wasn't expecting that!', 'Yuk', 'I'm not sure about this' and 'Will you stop me again?'
- The best communication with babies and toddlers picks up on these messages as you gaze and touch in your turn. Your words add the accompanying message of, 'And hello to you too!', 'Let's have a look together' or 'You didn't like that?'

Babies and toddlers are busy thinking; their body language, gestures and sound making show you that busy brain activity is going on. However, they cannot put thoughts into actual words yet.

A learning journey towards literacy

The learning journey over early childhood needs to lead towards recognisable literacy skills. However, the years of early childhood are all about building firm foundations through developmentally appropriate early years experiences. There has been a reprehensible level of pressure, especially within England, to fast-track young children into actual reading and writing. This serious problem is addressed in each of the other four books in this series. I raise it in this book as well, because deeply unwise practice sometimes enters the world of babies and young toddlers.

The following quotation from the EYFS Statutory Guidance applies across each of the six areas of learning and development and for every age range within early childhood.

It is crucial to their future success that children's earliest experiences help to build a secure foundation for learning throughout their school years and beyond. Practitioners must be sensitive to the individual development of each child to ensure that the activities they undertake are suitable for the stage they have reached. Children need to be stretched, but not pushed beyond their capabilities, so that they can continue to enjoy learning. (Page 10, paragraph 1.18.)

There is an unfortunate choice of words for the separate EYFS strands related to literacy, with headings like 'Linking sounds and letters' or 'Handwriting'. It is important that all practitioners realise that, for much of early childhood, good practice has absolutely nothing to do with letters of the alphabet or children producing handwriting. Early years practitioners are responsible for making sound developmental sense of this area and a focus on the earlier sections of the learning and development information will help. Firm foundations for literacy are built from a focus on skills and experiences in the following:

- Spoken, personal communication and the enjoyment of the give-and-take of authentic conversation – everything that has been covered in this section.
- Familiarity with singing and rhymes (see also page 56).
- Enjoyable mark-making which really does start in the baby year when they get their hands on materials (see page 53).
- Comfort in their own bodies and confidence to use physical skills in a deliberate way (see page 40).
- Time and playful support for imaginative play and the storytelling that flows from a pretend narrative (see page 53).
- A love of books and stories, supporting by many personal times when a book has been read or shared between a familiar adult and a very small number of children – group size limited to a sofa-full (see page 58).

Problem Solving, Reasoning and Numeracy

Problem solving and reasoning are not exclusively early mathematical skills – although numeracy would be placed in this broad category. The PSR part of PSRN has a great deal of common ground with the open-ended thinking which is part of the development of creativity. They are supported by the skills of communication, and frequently depend on use of physical dexterity. However, all the parts of PSRN may seem, at first sight, to be too intellectual or logical to have a place in the baby year. But, rather like the very beginnings of scientific thought, a great deal of early development is grounded in opportunities for babies and young toddlers to get their hands on a wide range of open-ended materials.

Look, listen and note/notice

In order to make sense of very young learning, you need to be alert to the small details of what babies and toddlers do, what interests them and how they use their senses to get a grip, usually in a very literal way, on the world around them. You also need to home in on what a particular aspect of development looks like in the early months and first year or so of life. This point has also been made about respect for the early communication skills of babies (see page 00).

Once you are attuned to looking at the baby version of problem solving or the toddler approach to early numeracy, then it is possible to observe all these developments within your days with babies and toddlers. Very young children make explorations, come to their own conclusions and are already aware of number or shape at the most basic, visual, get-my-hands-on-it level. Of course, babies and very young toddlers do not understand abstract number in the sense of 1, 2, 3. So it is pointless, and developmentally misleading, to buy commercial toys, books and wall friezes which feature single written numbers. However, babies notice differences in their familiar world. Their reactions and body language tell you they are aware that something has appeared or something else has gone.

For example

I observed many examples of the baby and toddler version of PSRN in my time in Southlands Crèche and in the under threes part of Grove House Children's Centre

- Older babies and toddlers were keen on songs and rhymes of all kinds, including the ones that include numbers for a good reason. In both settings, very young children experienced singing as a spontaneous activity and not always as a planned time.
- They enjoyed rhymes in which simple number words became familiar as part of a song and action sequence, as in touching and counting toes. Number words operated as a basic ordering of a sequence of actions in 'Round and round the garden' – a rhyme that is a continuing favourite.
- Obviously, babies and toddlers do not do calculations or measurement as such. But the mobile babies and toddlers in these nurseries did a great deal of enthusiastic exploration with their baskets of interesting

resources. There was a great deal of moving things about – following their own purposes. Over the days, toddlers tried a lot of random bringing materials together as they lifted items, put one into or on top of another and simply piled them.

- It was possible to see how they became familiar with resources and soon it really looked as if very young children had made a deliberate choice to pull out the ribbons this time, or to try putting the fir cones into a new container. The stop-and-look, as well as a certain amount of shove-it-and-see, could fairly be described as toddler estimating and guestimating.

Making direct contact

Babies need to build their first hand experiences and understanding of their world and to hone their physical skills. The abstract concepts of shape, space and spatial relationships cannot make any sense at all without these firm foundations of direct contact. As with any aspect of child development, you cannot look at PSRN in isolation from the rest of active baby learning.

For example

Babies work hard to gain control over their limbs and the rest of their body. When you are able to track developments over that first year or so of life, it becomes clear that 'normal' development is an impressive achievement. Over her baby year, Tanith's ability to control her own physical movements worked alongside the experiences we brought to her.

- By the end of her third month, Tanith was making what looked like deliberate movements to connect with an item, such as bashing her teddy bear with her fist. Using eyes and hands she was more able to close the gap between herself and something interesting.
- In her fourth month, Tanith developed a clear pattern of grabbing hold of toys. Her grip was strong enough that she was soon able to shake her lighter rattles. By the end of the month she was keen to be held upright, securely on my lap and to enjoy the different views that this position gave her.
- Over the second half of her baby year, Tanith used her physical skills to get hold of, explore and play with a wide range of items. She liked any kind of sound-making toy, like rattles and bells. She enjoyed having items in bags and baskets, which she could explore with her hands and pull out in whatever order she wished. Sitting securely on her bottom and slightly bent legs, Tanith was at that point for older babies that Elinor Goldschmied described as having 'time on their hands'.
- By the end of her baby year, Tanith had a wide repertoire of play. She loved any version of peep-boo - when we covered our faces, but she also learned to cover herself and then pull off the cloth. She loved bags and putting things in and out again. She put bits of lego into a box and then rattled them around. Part of her play started to include a proper two handed clap, which joined her active wave, for goodbye or goodnight.
- Tanith always relished lively, physical play. As she approached her first birthday, her preferences were for a great deal of whole body movement – climbing over us, being chased by crawling, lots of tickling and cuddling. Tanith discovered by direct physical engagement all the spatial relationships of over, under, through and on top of.
- She enjoyed our weekly session at the Roly-Poly Club, an informal parent and child drop-in where she moved around at speed on the cushioned surfaces.
- She was a keen climber and, before she was able to walk, had mastered a confident clamber onto a leather pouffe and was able to use her own wooden chair as the means to get closer to items she could not otherwise reach.

Food for thought

Baby and toddler understanding of shape is led through their physical exploration of interesting three-dimensional objects which they can feel, lift, carry around, pile up and put into containers. They feel and see curves and edges. They explore what will fit inside and what will not, no matter how hard they push it.

Babies' grasp of space is very direct. Space is experienced as a personal issue – cuddling up close so that there is no space between you or covering the intervening space at speed, by crawling or toddling in order to close that gap.

If you care for babies more than a couple of months old you will notice that many can be uneasy or distressed if the open space around them looks 'too big and empty'. Prior to birth they have spent their life in an increasingly snug space. So it is not surprising that young babies often prefer to be wrapped up, or to feel the comforting boundaries of your arms. Some definitely like to feel the edge of a baby bath with their feet and, without this edge to their world, may show a startled reaction by flinging up their hands and arms.

Being a helpful adult

Active older babies, especially once they can move themselves around, are enthusiastic explorers of their immediate world. They need a generous supply of simple materials and then they are very engaged in bringing items together in different ways:

- They like placing objects or turning them around and looking, often quite hard and from different angles.
- They have the physical skills to put the same object in different places into different containers and to drop or start to throw things, just to see what happens.
- They have a lot of fun with repetitive games in which you roll a ball away from you both and they crawl or totter after it, finding where the ball has gone this time and trying to bring it back.
- Helpful adults tune into the importance of these repetitive games, noticing that each run of the game is not exactly the same. Older babies and toddlers need adult assistance for some of the physical skills to keep this kind of game going, or the ability to direct or aim a ball, soft cube or other safe rolling or flying object.

- Physical play is often the way that babies and young toddlers start to experience the sense of space that is about close to, further away and closing a gap between the two of us. As an older baby, Tanith liked crawling-chasing (one of us on all fours as well as her) just as much as her brother had earlier. Once she was confidently mobile as a young toddler, she loved being chased in play, often by her brother Drew.

Babies and toddlers as young scientists

Babies begin to problem solve and exercise control over their familiar world by having the time to explore how things work. Again here is a reminder that of course the six areas of learning and development in the EYFS are inter-connected – PSRN relates closely to babies' growing knowledge and understanding of their world.

For example

In Southlands Crèche a great deal of thought and planning has gone into creating a relaxed day for the babies and very young toddlers in the small groups that make up this provision. Joanne and Claire, who run the baby room team, go out in the local neighbourhood every day (see the example on page 37). Time spent indoors is unhurried and takes account of the different personal routines of individual babies. Within the flow of the day there is still generous time for these babies and young toddlers to explore a wide range of open-ended materials.

On several winter time visits (in summer the group is out in the garden much more) I observed many occasions when a mobile baby was able to drive their own learning through the resources they chose.

- During one afternoon, Tammy, a very young toddler, was obviously enjoying a book, comfortable and snuggled up to Joanne. Tammy looked closely at the book and already understood how to turn the pages. She was also able and keen to put the book back into the container (a low wooden open storage system) and choose another book by herself.

- Charlie (14 months) was made welcome to join with the impromptu story time with Joanne and Tammy. But he was busy exploring the large collection of plastic bottles. Something different had been placed in each bottle and the top made secure. Charlie selected bottles in a deliberate way and one at a time. He experimented with what they would do and discovered that some bottles made a sound, sometimes a rattle. Charlie repeated his actions, looking and listening carefully. The contents of some bottles moved around more than others and a vigorous shaking brought about much shifting of the materials inside.
- A low mirror in the room enabled babies and toddlers to look at themselves and others in reflection. For some time Charlie intently watched himself in the process of shaking different bottles.
- Despite his concentration on exploring the bottles, Charlie continued to be aware of the adults in the room. More than once, he looked across to Joanne, who was able to show her interest with a smile and show that she definitely had kept Charlie in mind. I had become a familiar face in the room and at one point Charlie looked at me and smiled, as I watched him try different ways of making sounds.

Very early understanding of amount

The beginnings of really early numeracy are intertwined with a growing understanding of the world around what is familiar and what is unfamiliar.

- Even very young babies show an awareness of what is well known and what is new. Sometimes they will stare for longer at a visual sight that is new to them – although they do not tire of gazing at the familiar face of their parent or their key person in out of home care.
- Something familiar can be experienced by a baby as potentially interesting – worth reaching out to touch and grasp. Sometimes their facial expression and body language tells you, 'This may be interesting. But I'm not sure – so stay close to me.' Sometimes, a sight or sound sensation is too strong or sudden for this baby or young toddler and they show distress.
- Within the second half of the first year, babies reach the significant understanding that objects can be temporarily out of sight, but are not gone forever. This concept of object permanence is a big intellectual step.

For example

You can watch Orson, in *The Wonder Year* (Siren Films) who, at seven months, is interested in a ball game with his mother. She hides the ball under a cushion and Orson is able to see her do this, but he does not search for the ball, although he has been enjoying their game. At nine months, Orson's understanding has taken a leap. When Mum hides a doll under a cloth as Orson watches he immediately grabs hold of the cloth and pulls it off the doll. His mother hides it again and Orson confidently reveals the doll a second time.

It is easy for practitioners working with three- and four-year-olds to overlook how much young children are 'doing and thinking maths' through the flow of their chosen play and their involvement in daily routines like laying the table or tidying up play resources. Adults are sometimes looking for something too complicated and abstract in terms of grasp of number. So it can be even more perplexing to consider that babies' alertness to their world leads them into an awareness of amount and very basic numeracy.

Being a helpful adult

In a family home or home of a childminder there will often be some mixing across the age range of early childhood. In a group setting, babies and toddlers are very likely to be in a different base room to the slightly older children. I have observed good practice in a range of nurseries where that has been recognition of the great advantage of easing contact between the ages. Teams have ensured a way of organising that brings the ages together sometimes.

Some older children (but still under fives), boys as well as girls, really enjoy the role of play assistant to a baby or toddler in the types of games described in this section.

- Listen and watch out for babies whose reaction shows you they have noticed that one item has gone missing. They have a first idea of number or amount in terms of what was there just a moment ago. Perhaps they have been momentarily distracted and, when they turn back, one of their collection of little containers has gone, or another little brush has joined their collection.
- Their sounds of surprise or a puzzled expression communicates the message that would be said out loud by, 'Hold on! There wasn't that many last time I looked!'
- When toddlers start to speak, some of the early words are about amount - personal words like 'nomore', 'allgone', 'onemore' and 'na'one'.
- Older babies and young toddlers often show enjoyment at the anticipation of physical fun that starts with 'One, two, three – go!' Some young toddlers start to echo that pattern of sound in order to provoke a familiar adult into this happy exchange of being lifted up, gently swung or to run and leap into your outstretched arms.
- Long before babies or very young toddlers will use the actual words, familiar adults will be commenting on what you and the baby can see: your shared focus of attention. As you sit on the grass together you will enjoy looking at the birds. 'Ooh look', accompanied by pointing is an appropriate time to say, 'There's a bird… Ooh there's another bird... over there… two birds.'
- Alison Gopnik (2009) describes research studies that have shown how older babies not only look very carefully, but also make sense of their observations in terms of 'how much' or 'more' of one thing than another. In one experiment nine-month-old babies were shown a box full of ping pong balls, of which 80% were red and 20% were white. A screen was then put in front of the box and an adult picked out five balls of the same colour. The babies definitely looked longer at these balls when they were all white. Their observation of the mainly red box seemed to lead them to a sense of, 'That's rather unlikely'. Their reaction was not about the colour itself. If the adult took five red, or white, ping pong balls out of a pocket, then the babies did not look at the white set for any longer than usual.
- Mealtimes with older babies and young toddlers are appropriate times to be saying, 'Would you like some more grated cheese?' or 'I bet you can eat two carrot sticks.'

Hands-on exploration

Babies need a rich array of safe materials that they can act upon and organise in ways that interest them today. What works is very simple as some commercially produced toys are over-manufactured. For instance, babies and young toddlers are interested in shape as a quality to feel, and they are keen to engage in a great deal of putting in and taking out. They also like to do a lot of what I call piling and filing – a very personal approach to organising and re-organising a generous supply of items that they can seize one at a time.

You will meet the developmental needs of babies and young toddlers when you ensure that they have plenty of simple materials which they can explore in their own way. You will always be close enough so that they cannot come to harm, for instance by what they manage to get into their mouth. The resource called the 'Treasure Basket' was developed by Elinor Goldschmied several decades ago, and promoted with the support of fellow early years specialists, especially Anita Hughes (2006). Over the 1970s and 1980s Elinor Goldschmied was concerned about the serious intrusion of plastic toys into a child's world. This situation has become significantly worse since she first warned that young children need materials to engage all five senses: hearing, vision, touch, smell and taste. Elinor Goldschmied also identified a 'sixth sense': young children's sensitivity to their own bodily movement and recognition of what physical skills feel like when they are used.

The whole point of the Treasure Basket, for babies who are able to sit securely, is that they can select, pick up and explore from a large collection of items presented in a low, open basket.

- The aim is to avoid any commercially made toys or plastic, since this material is so dominant in bought play materials.
- There are no other firm rules for the contents of a treasure basket, except that there should be a large quantity of items. The aim is to have a full basket, so that an older baby or toddler can rout through it, picking and discarding some items and deciding which one(s) are worthy of their full attention today.
- The materials should be able to be wiped clean and no object should be so small that babies or toddlers could swallow it.
- You collect ordinary objects that are safe for babies to handle and mouth. You may have small containers – some with lids and some without – and perhaps there is an object inside a container with a firm lid.
- You can have large cotton reels, woolly balls, a firm fruit like a lemon (regularly replaced), a wooden spoon or spatula, little metal bowls or sieves which can be seized by small hands, large, unvarnished wooden curtain rings, a bath sponge, a small scoop or pastry cutters, old fashioned clothes pegs (without the spring system) which are often called dolly pegs, little brushes, a purse, and so on.
- The collection should vary in look, texture, shape, sound-making quality and smell, so that babies can explore in any way they wish.

The idea is that an adult is close by the Treasure Basket, but that the adult simply looks attentive. An older baby or young toddler, sometimes one sitting on either side of the basket, is free to explore the contents in whatever way they like. You neither plan nor direct how the resource is used. The babies themselves make choices: so you should not suggest or offer particular materials. There is no need to comment on what the babies are doing, nor to intervene unless there is a genuine safety issue. However, you do not remain silent, because you respond to anything that a baby or toddler wants to show you.

Food for thought

The problem with many commercially produced shape sorter toys aimed at under twos is that the physical task of fitting up to five or six different three-dimensional shapes to the right hole is far too difficult.

I have watched many older babies and young toddlers with these toys. Whenever there is a lid to a posting box, they take it off and neatly simplify the task to fit their current skill level. The older baby or toddler then has a fine time putting any shape into the container, taking it out again, rattling the container with shapes inside, tipping them out again and so on.

They are happy to use a simple lid with an all-purpose posting gap, into which a wide range of items can be eased. This age group is ready to explore the simpler ideas of size around 'big' and 'little', along with a direct experience of 'too big', when something will not post through the gap.

Being a helpful adult

I could have placed this section about the Treasure Basket within any of the six areas of learning. The same point applies to the entire concept of hands-on exploratory play for babies and toddlers.

The EYFS, like any other developmentally-based early years guidance, stresses the crucial importance of children choosing their own materials, organising themselves in ways that make sense for their age and initiating their own play. Adults are supportive play companions, happily watching and following the lead of a baby, toddler or child. It is developmentally poor practice to try to micro-manage a day through adult control of which resources will be made available this morning – let alone deciding in advance what babies will be encouraged to do with materials or trying to predict exactly what this baby or toddler will gain from the experience.

Adults are really important for babies. You, and your colleagues if you work in a team, are the people who ensure that a Treasure Basket, often more than one in a nursery, is well stocked and easily available. Your organisation, creativity and imagination are all needed to create an interesting and accessible physical environment. Keep the resources simple and then follow the lead set by a baby or toddler for the level of complexity they establish in their play.

Thoughtful early years practitioners realise that sitting peaceably close to a baby with a Treasure Basket can seem hard when you start to offer this resource. It may seem as if, 'I'm not doing anything' or 'Shouldn't I say something'. However, this is a special time of quiet concentration – for you just as much as for the baby or toddler. There will be plenty of times in a day when you chat with babies and comment. Now is an excellent chance to watch and learn more about this individual baby or young toddler.

- What interests them today? What items are they choosing to touch and pick up?
- What are they doing with the item and which senses are they bringing to bear?
- What does their face tell you - do they look surprised or puzzled?
- Babies cannot put their discoveries into spoken words for you. So this time of companionable observation is vital. You relax into the flow of what is happening in front of you today and reflect on what have you learned today about what this baby or toddler has probably discovered.

For example

Readers who are familiar with the Treasure Basket will have their own observations which highlight memorable moments when the chosen actions of a baby 'speak' about what they must surely be thinking. Visual materials from DVDs can help this process.

- There is a magic moment in the *Key Times* DVD developed by Julia Manning-Morton and Maggie Thorp (2006) when a baby picks up and mouths a loofah. A doubtful expression passes over his face – not quite distaste but close to that expression. But the baby mouths the loofah again until it looks as if he has confirmed, for himself, that this odd taste and feel is definitely linked with this item.
- Jamie, aged seven months in *Exploratory Play* from Siren (2006) picks up and shakes a number of items, in some cases also seeing what happens if they are banged against the edge of the basket. Jamie also appears to be unimpressed by the taste of at least one item.

The Treasure Basket, as envisaged by Elinor Goldschmied, is intended for babies who are not yet easily moving about to organise their own use of resources. The principle of interesting collections of items remains important once young toddlers become confidently mobile. The approach of 'lots and lots of stuff' is brought to life by the Heuristic Play sessions, developed by Elinor Goldschmied and Anita Hughes for day nurseries or any other group provision for children.

- For a nursery, crèche or drop-in centre, you need to gather a wide range of materials so that there will be more than enough for a small group of toddlers. A similar resource for home use could be one large bag or box of materials. The materials are similar to the treasure basket: natural materials rather than bought toys.
- For instance, you will be able to collect many different types and size of container, with and without lids. Cardboard or see-through tubes have many uses. Safe lengths of metal chain, empty cones from knitting machine wool, old-fashioned wooden clothes pegs, large corks, large sponge hair curlers, large wooden curtain rings and other everyday and recycled natural materials.
- You need to store the play materials in large cloth bags or similar containers that will keep the material dust-free and safe. You can bring out the materials once or twice a week as a special play time, so that the resource does not become over familiar.
- You lay out the material attractively in a clear space and let toddlers play and explore as they wish. As with the Treasure Basket, the idea is that adults relax, look at, and enjoy anything that toddlers wish to show you, or with which they want your help.
- Resist the temptation to direct the exploration or talk at the toddlers about what they are doing. Just follow their play with your eyes and ears and become no more involved than they want you to.
- Tidying up is part of the exploration and learning. You need to plan the timing so that toddlers and very young children are not rushed. They will enjoy feeling competent and responsible as they help you put all the materials back into the bags for the next heuristic play session.

This kind of open-ended exploratory play can be reflected in how you choose to resource the physical environment as a whole for mobile young toddlers. In fact, the approach of the Treasure Basket or of Heuristic Play should absolutely not be small islands in a sea of otherwise adult-dominated and pre-planned activities. When babies and toddlers have easy access to open-ended materials, then you are able to see their current, preferred ways of acting upon their world. Babies are in the process of honing their physical skills and over the first year of life they steadily build the ability to use hands and fingers to get hold of items (see the discussion on page 25).

Once young toddlers have confident control and mobility, then you can see how they repeat sequences of action out of choice and sometimes they persist, for some time, in a particular way of exploring and organising their world. These repeated patterns are called schemas and examples could be that an individual toddler becomes very interested in filling up containers with different items, possibly carrying these around from place to place. Another toddler, with or without a friend, may become absorbed day after day in covering and uncovering himself or play items, in wrapping paper or cloth around toys or his own feet. Attentive adults will be able to see problem solving in young toddlers' exploration of cause and effect, materials that fit and those that do not, materials that operate as effective wraps or covers, and those which are just not up to the job.

For example

- *Exploratory Play* from Siren (2006) provides the useful opportunity to see Jamie again, at 23 months, when she organises a generous supply of containers, curtain rings and other items. It is possible to see Jamie deliberately lining up items, setting out the rings carefully in a pattern and placing single rings into single containers in a visual explanation of one-to-one correspondence.

Food for Thought

The importance of hands-on exploration does not fade away after the very earliest years. A generous supply of open-ended materials continues to be the way that practitioners can best support children's use of their skills of problem solving and creative thinking.

The House of Objects is an innovative resource developed in North Tyneside and made available to children and young adolescents. You can watch a short DVD on http://childrenfirst.northtyneside.gov.uk/article/?id=85067 and read more about the project on http://www.northtyneside.gov.uk/pls/portal/NTC_PSCM.PSCM_Web.download?p_ID=224273

Do use this material to reflect on the continuity of good practice with the very youngest throughout childhood. The underlying principle of what you should offer does not change; the details vary. For instance, wise adults think carefully about what babies and toddlers can get their hands on, because most items will go into their mouth. Observant adults notice that as the months and years pass, what children do with 'lots of stuff' changes along with their physical skills and personal store of knowledge.

Knowledge and Understanding of the World

This area of learning and development within the EYFS is divided into the strands of 'exploration and investigation', 'designing and making', 'ICT', 'time', 'place' and 'communities'. All of these aspects are of potential relevance to babies and young toddlers. However, a proper focus on child development has to be led by familiar adults who are committed to learning about and tuning into the personal and social world of really young children.

A baby's world does not need artificial stimulation

Until babies are able to move themselves you have to bring items of interest to them or take them in your arms to interesting sights. In a suitable physical environment for ones, they are able to see possibilities and eye-point them out to you, even before they can use the power of finger pointing. Babies are programmed to explore, to strive to use their physical skills, however limited those may seem within the early weeks and months. Neural connections within the brain are made when babies engage directly with their world using all their senses. They want to do or experience something again, and again, and again. Happy repetition is perfect for building those connections and for ensuring that practice makes better.

Babies are ready to find their world of great interest. The real world is fascinating; it does not have to be made more 'stimulating' for babies with commercial toys that increase the amount of random noise and create an unnatural world dominated by primary colours, rather than shades and tones. Babies lead their explorations through their senses. So a major drawback to an environment dominated by plastic toys is that they offer an impoverished sensory experience to babies or children.

Firm moulded plastic as a material has become very common in many commercially produced toys for babies and young children. It is easy for unreflective adults – practitioners as well as parents – to think that this situation is fine and normal, when shelves are full of plastic toys in primary colours. The natural world is not dominated by bright red, blue, green and yellow. Look around outside; there are many shades, pastel as well as primary colours and so many different kinds of green or brown. A young child's world needs subtle shades and neutrals, and then brighter colours become of interest sometimes.

Plastic has limited interest by touch – it is smooth but cannot be bent or changed. It usually has no smell, taste or texture. Many such toys have a visual overload, since so much is fixed to the toy. The appeal to sound is also often overloaded as buttons release different pre-recorded noises, words or snatches of song. Furthermore, unlike a basket of ribbons or a collection of little boxes, it is not possible for babies or toddlers to get hold of one thing at a time, or a couple if they wish. They have no choice but to engage with the whole moulded plastic toy. For instance, they cannot remove the bit that does the bell so that they can explore the bell and ringing with intense baby concentration.

Sensory exploration and investigation

Of all the senses, smell is sometimes overlooked. However, like the other senses, smells are directly experienced by babies and the messages transmitted to their brain as electrical signals, like any other information they encounter in their world. Experience of smells, and their associations with people, routines and events – are logged in the infant brain, along with the associated feelings. It used to be thought that a sense of smell requires air and breathing. But there is now good reason to believe that in the womb a foetus reacts to different smells within the amniotic fluid. It seems that, like other senses, the sense of smell can operate in this liquid environment.

Newborns react to smells and are drawn towards the smell of breast milk. Part of their sense of familiarity with known adults is about how you smell (in the nicest possible way of course!). For babies, smells soon become associated with routines, rather than just milk and then food.

- For example, older babies often develop a strong attachment to an object, such as a muslin square, a blanket or a particular soft toy. The smell of this much loved object is as important as how it looks and feels.
- Your only hope is to wash it regularly from the outset – which may not be possible, because a baby and then toddler will not let it go. Woe betide you if you wash it later, because you will remove the crucial smell.
- As I discovered, the exact feel can be just as important. I foolishly decided to mend the frayed corner of my young son's baby quilt, which had become his toddler comfort object. His aghast expression, let alone the wails, let me know that I had ruined a key feature of the quilt. I had to unpick all my careful stitching and restore the corner to its tatty state.

Taste also seems to be activated in the womb and is an important sense from early infancy. Our sense of taste actually works together with the sense of smell. The taste buds on our tongue can distinguish four basic qualities: sweet, sour, bitter and salt. Any other tastes and subtle variations are detected by the receptors located high up in our nasal passage. The sensory receptors in a baby's mouth are the most sensitive of all and they gain a great deal of information by mouthing objects. As well as any taste to an object, a baby's mouth also tells them about the feel, the texture of an object. It is a hopeless task to try to stop babies or toddlers putting items into their mouth; you just have to ensure that everything is safe.

The sense of feeling, of touch, is activated as a foetus moves around, with steadily less space as the months go by. The importance of continued touch for newborns has been shown by how twin babies sometimes want to be close to each other. The physical presence of the stronger twin may reassure a baby sibling who still needs to be in the intensive care unit. Depending on the circumstances, medical staff may encourage the babies to be placed together, for at least some time, while an adult is beside the cot. However, the general advice on safety is not to place babies together in a cot to sleep, unless the adult is awake and observant. There is a risk that a physically active baby could roll on top of their sibling.

The sense of touch and being touched, often combines with the sense of movement. Babies often like to be rocked, perhaps accompanied by singing or gentle talk. They often like to feel the sensations of being on the move, walked around or in a pram or buggy. Over infancy, it will be many months before human babies manage any kind of independent mobility. It is possible that their most basic survival instinct tells them that being held close and moved means that they are safe and are not abandoned to the predators. In contrast with other mammals, human newborns are highly vulnerable; contrast them with newborn lambs or deer. They get to their

Food for Thought

Babies' eyesight is especially sensitive to the sharp contrasts of black and white. It is developmentally appropriate to ensure that you have an array of materials in black and white – see the example on page 00.

You might create a special corner with a varied store of materials that are mainly black and white and tones. Or you could have a special basket of such materials. You can also make mobiles by using paper plates and drawing on them with a thick, black felt tip. You might draw solid shapes or simple patterns.

It is useful for practitioners and parents to be aware of babies' great interest in black and white. This knowledge may also help to reduce the overwhelming use of primary colours across a room for babies or toddlers. However, you do not of course turn their whole indoor environment into an exclusive black and white zone.

feet – wobbly but upright – and their continued survival requires them to move with their mother. She will protect them as best possible, but does not carry her babies.

Vision is operating as a sense from pre-birth and early infancy, but a newborn's range for sharp focus is no more than the distance to the face of someone who is holding the baby in their arms. Some of the footage in the DVD *Baby it's you* (see page 63) shows the fuzzy edges of the personal world of a young baby. If you watch young babies you will see how they stare at objects and people who are within their clear visual range.

For example

- By two to three weeks old Tanith was showing sustained interest in objects within close visual range. She stared especially at a black and white panda cuddly toy, at lights and directly at the big eyes of a rag doll.
- Her interest in human faces led to some intent staring, and by seven weeks she was also intrigued by the large clock in the living room.
- During her third month, she looked intently at different objects: favourites were the pictures on her cloth cube, the dangling items on a cradle gym and one particular rattle that had a face on one side and mirror on the other side.

Hearing also has become active before birth. There is plenty of support now for saying that babies can hear sounds from the outside while they are still in the womb. Newborns show an alert reaction to voices, like that of their mother, which they have heard many times. They also sometimes show a reaction of familiarity or reassurance to songs or music, which they have heard before birth. Human babies are poised to be attentive to the sounds of the human voice and the rhythm of spoken language. Around the world, they are soothed by singing and they have what Colwyn Trevarthen has called a quality of musicality to their own sound making and the flow of what they like to hear. (See page 17 about the rhythm of infant directed speech.)

For example

- My own daughter, Tanith, certainly looked alert as a very young baby when she heard her brother's favourite rhymes and songs. More to the point, Tanith was hearing them again, since 'Miss Polly' and 'There was a cottage in the wood' would have travelled through to her many times before she was born.
- However, Tanith soon developed firm favourites of her own, as I tried out other songs I had learned from my consultancy work in day nurseries. By three months of age, her top favourite was 'Hello Aunt Jemima', which the practitioners believed to be an old music hall song.

First hand experiences and the thrill of discovery

Babies and toddlers – and children as a whole – need first hand experiences. They need a rich array of open-ended resources and plenty of scope to determine for themselves the direction of an activity that interests them. If practitioners are tempted to pre-package and over-organise experiences, there is far less potential for babies or children to be active themselves and to extend their current understanding of the world.

Any play resource needs to have generous possibilities and that it can be used in different ways, combined with other items. The serious problem with many commercial produced toys is that the possibilities have already been severely limited. The moulded 'early learning' table or stand cannot be taken apart. There is no point in making sounds to and on behalf of the dolly or teddy, because a push on their stomach releases a stream of pre-recorded comments.

For example

I was made welcome by Donna Fletcher at a World of Discovery session at the Flagship Centre in Tilbury. This project across Thurrock has offered sessions for babies and parents equipped with many open-ended resources. In this session, the materials were mainly black and white, but otherwise varied in size, feel and sound-making properties.

All the babies were happily absorbed for most of the hour long session, some for the full amount of time. They were able to move around and find different items from the generous display available on the floor. All the babies spent some time on each item of their own choosing. Their parents (in this session they were all mothers) and Donna were present all the time and there was a soft background of quiet musical sounds.

- Jon, a nine month old boy, grasped with both hands a large square of dark cellophane. He pulled his hands back and forth, grasping on tight, and listened as the material made a rustling sound. Jon let it drop – the action looked deliberate – and then it picked it up again.
- Then he rolled on the cellophane and wrapped himself up in it. From his face, it looked as if this had not been deliberate. However, Jon was not distressed (his mother was close by in any case). He just looked interested in what he had managed to do.
- The babies in this session definitely looked interested in each other. At one point Jon rolled confidently over onto all fours and looked intently at a sitting baby, close to him. He reached out and gently touched her foot. She in turn reached out equally gently and touched Jon's face.
- Other babies in the session sometimes halted in their physical explorations in order to watch what another baby was doing. Sometimes they vocalised to each other; sometimes their varied sound-making was aimed at the adults.
- A younger baby lay on her back contentedly and held a large square of white organza – staring at the material, feeling it when it dropped to her face and experiencing the texture from her strong grasp on the edges.

In the second session, the children were mainly of toddler age and were able to explore the same array of materials as the previous group of babies.

- One really liked the dark net hanging curtains and played several rounds of peek-a-boo.
- Another little boy spent absorbed time with a length of black plastic chain and a large white bowl. He pulled the chain up to its full length – he was able to do this action because he was

Being a helpful adult

Practical implications of the research about buggies need to be taken with care.

- Wheeled equipment does not work communication magic. Experiences for babies depend on what people do – the equipment with the legs and a voice! A towards-facing buggy cannot itself be more emotionally healthy for the baby.
- Certainly I have now seen too many adults talking on their mobile phone, while pushing a torward-facing buggy. Those babies learn that they are far less important than the magic box in the adult's hand, and toddlers that they are insignificant compared with whoever is on the other end.
- The key issue is that communication is part of this outing. If babies are in a towards-facing buggy, then you can chat with them on the trip, whilst being alert to where you are going.
- If you have outward-facing buggies, then you need to stop regularly, get to the baby or toddler's level, look together and chat. A towards-facing buggy will have to be turned on occasion, so older babies can look in the same direction as you.
- The buggy style to avoid has to be the two-level double buggy style, in which one baby or child is tucked away in the lower section, with few options of talking with anyone, or seeing what on earth is happening around them.

standing up – and dropped it into the bowl. The chain made a very satisfying rattling sound and he repeated this action several times.

- One toddler was held up by an adult so he could make contact with the pompoms suspended from the ceiling. He hit them and watched as they swung behind his head and then back round again. He repeated the action several times, looking fascinating by this movement.

Kaylee, an eight month old girl, was active with many materials.

- She had a fine time with the cellophane. Kaylee was able to sit securely and she really pulled the cellophane about, making it rustle loudly. She waved it up and down, again and again vigorously, yet did not tip from her sitting position.
- Then Kaylee became interested in the base of the black and white box. She held it with one, and then two hands, then waved it around, dropped it and hit it.
- Kaylee then moved herself from the sitting position to get moving. She used a successful hump and pull strategy and got herself across the soft quilt covering to reach other items that had caught her eye.
- Over her time in the session, Kaylee spent her energy on a store of tissue paper and a black and white dumbbell shape that she could squeeze, rattle, hold, shake and squeeze again.
- She showed great interest in a laminated black and white pattern within a circle. Kaylee looked closely, shook and bent the laminated item. She then held it firmly on each side and banged it against her legs, making a different sound.

Time and place in a baby's world

Time for babies is very much about personal timing and happy routines within the shape of a day. Over the baby year and into the toddler months, they begin to understand and welcome the familiarity of routines, so long as time and timing supports intimate physical care and babies do not feel rushed or harassed. Young babies start to recognise the sounds, smells or adult preparations that mean that mealtime or bathtime is about to start. The timing and sequence in a nappy change should be a personal experience and a time of warm communication. So, long before clock time, days or seasons have any meaning at all, babies get a feel for 'what happens here' and 'what that means for me'.

Until mobile, toddlers can walk at least short distance on an outing, babies will travel from place to place in a buggy, unless they are strapped or wrapped to your body. Babies need to feel fully engaged in the experience of going out

land about. Buggies are a fine invention, but it is important that the equipment does not end up creating an emotional distance between the baby and the adult.

Suzanne Zeedyk carried out research into how adults communicate with babies, depending on the style of buggy that was used. She looked at babies and toddlers (under twos) and found that parents tended to talk more to the infants when they were sat in a buggy that faced the adult (what the research called the toward-facing style of buggy). The study raises important issues about what may encourage adults – practitioners as well as the parents in this study – to chat with babies and very young children as a normal part of the daily routine.

An understanding of personal time and place is also supported by regular, frequent experiences of going out and about in the local community. Babies and young toddlers can get to know a familiar neighbourhood, start to recognise the last corner before you reach the market and get excited because part of this outing is that you always buy some fruit from this stall.

For example

In the Southlands Crèche in Newcastle-Under-Lyme, Joanne Gallimore and Claire Hollins are committed to getting out every day with the babies into the neighbourhood. It has to be seriously unfriendly weather to stop them.

- Sometimes Joanne and Claire make the walk into the nearby town centre and the babies and young toddlers experience interesting events of ordinary life, such as buying vegetables from the market.
- They regularly get out to the local park, enjoying a picnic in warmer weather. There is relaxed time to look at the flowers, watch the birds and listen to the sounds of the outdoors.
- Of course, babies and very young toddlers sometimes fall asleep in their buggy – that is a normal event – and some restless babies are very soothed by the movement of travelling along, as well as friendly chat to them.
- In partnership with parents, Joanne and Claire sometimes make the trip to the local clinic for babies to be weighed.
- The crèche has been located here for some time and the staff group is stable. Consequently, Joanne and Claire have come to know many people who live locally. Part of a normal outing is that they stop and chat with, or are greeted by, familiar adults. The babies and toddlers experience that they too are part of this local community.
- The Crèche uses the toward-facing buggies for babies and toddlers up to about 18 months of age. Joanne and Claire judge that it is best for these very young children to face them and enjoy eye contact and friendly chat.
- Older toddlers, who will usually have moved into the next crèche age group, are encouraged to walk short distances. When they use buggies, these are outward-facing, so that toddlers can see directly what is coming up on the trip today.

I agree with this switch to outward-facing buggies, since toddlers and young children need to see around them and to spot interesting sights that are coming into view. Babies and toddlers become steadily more familiar with their immediate neighbourhood. This kind of support for knowledge and understanding of a familiar world is continued, in different ways, by the team members who are responsible for twos and over threes.

Fran Connell, the owner/manager of Southlands Kindergarten and Crèche, has always been adamant that the main objective should be to create a home-like feel. The overall aim is to offer the same kind of appropriate experiences that families share with their children. Official guidance has,

Food for thought

in some ways, finally caught up with this early years setting – with the focus on a home-like model in the EYFS Statutory Guidance (look back at page 9 for the relevant quotation).

The wording from the Foundation Stage KUW strand was changed for the EYFS from the phrase 'cultures and beliefs' to using the word 'communities'. This change may well support early years practitioners to focus properly on the perspective of a young child. 'Culture' is a broad and complex idea and only makes sense during early childhood when you approach it through the immediate personal and social world of very young children.

Babies and young toddlers experience a sense of community through their immediate environment. When you share the care of young children, part of your responsibility is to understand who and what is significant in this baby or toddler's personal and social world. Who is in their family; immediate and extended? Who has become familiar to them, including while they are in your care? This question includes other babies and children as well as important adults, such as their key person.

Experience of the natural world

Babies and young toddlers are fascinated by the sights and sounds of the natural world and, with a little bit of care, they can be brought into direct contact, as well as what they experience by being taken out and about into local open spaces.

For example

I enjoyed talking with Carole Allen and Ellen Edwards, both childminders in the Charlton area of south London. They have been actively involved in the development of the Greenwich Forest School project in their neighbourhood. When we met in early summer 2009, Ellen was part way through her training as a forest school leader.

- Carole and Ellen were already committed to getting out with their children on a daily basis into the local open spaces. Getting the very youngest children out on a regular basis is partly about attitudes; when practitioners value all the learning from outdoors, then they make it happen.
- They pointed out that it is inevitably time consuming to get babies and young toddlers all ready to get out, especially when colder weather requires a lot of wrapping up to keep warm. It is important to see this time as part of the routine and not a reason to avoid going outside.
- There will often be paths within the more organised landscape of urban parks. However, the less organised outdoor world is often not easily accessible with a buggy. The point of the Forest School experience is that wooded and other natural areas are enjoyed.

Carole and Ellen have successfully taken babies as young as eight and nine months with them into their wooded Forest School site.

- Sometimes babies can travel on your back, in a suitable carrier; sometimes they are carried in your arms.
- A small amount of planning means that even babies can enjoy the experience. Carole and Ellen take a rug or similar covering, so that babies can be safe on the forest floor. They sit with them and make a careful choice of natural materials for older babies to touch and explore.
- Consequently, the slightly older children in their care are not denied this time, on the grounds that it is all too complicated when you have babies as well.

Developmental common sense over ICT

Children in the UK now live in a highly technological world and eventually they need to become technologically literate, including using computers. This particular learning journey does not have to start in the earliest years, especially if adult choice of toys moves babies away from direct engagement of real objects and authentic experiences. Information and Communication Technology is a broad term and includes everyday technology, from domestic equipment to technology used within the local environment. There is no obligation to use computer-related technology with young children, and responsible early years practitioners need to be very wary about some of the claims on products aimed at the earliest years of childhood.

As each year passes, the toy industry produces more electronic products and extends the range of DVDs marketed for the full early childhood age group, including babies. There are several key problems with these products:

- Many claim to promote an understanding of concepts that are well beyond the potential understanding of the target age group.
- It is common for companies to claim that use of their simple laptop display product or DVD set will help under ones with abstract concepts like colour or number. Yet, these are babies who have not yet worked out the symbolic nature of language applied to familiar objects and people.

There is good reason to advise responsible adults to restrict screen time for young children – whatever the content or format of the equipment. They do not benefit from hours of sitting still in front of a television or computer screen. This advice is even more urgent when babies are involved. Even the more wakeful babies sleep for many hours. Their waking time should be spent with real people, who talk and listen, provide open-ended play resources that enable babies to decide on their own explorations and active play opportunities (see page 27) that cannot possibly be delivered by a screen.

(see page 27)

Food for thought

In family homes, where the television is simply left on all the time, adults appear to talk less in total to young children, regardless of whether anyone is actually watching the screen. The equipment provides a kind of sound and visual wallpaper. Nobody is really taking much notice of it, but the impact on eyes and ears is enough to interrupt the attention of very young children. The problem is also that they become accustomed to ignoring sounds.

I recall talking with a team of home visitors, who aimed to support play within the home. An early objective was always to encourage a parent to switch off the television, at least for the duration of the visit. I heard the same considered view from speech and language therapists who did home visits.

Physical Development

Over the first year of life, assuming that nothing happens to disrupt the flow of normal development, babies make breathtaking progress in terms of their ability to recognise and control their own body and to move themselves around a familiar environment. Human babies are highly vulnerable because they cannot move themselves away from risky situations and have no understanding anyway of what might be a danger to their well being. They are, however, highly motivated to use their current physical skills and bodily strength to the best of their ability.

Babies need to be able to move

Babies initially have limited active control over their arms and legs. They need to be supported in your arms because they cannot hold their head, which is relatively large and heavy, in proportion to the rest of their body. Over the early weeks and months their muscle control moves from the top of the body downwards and from the midline of their body outwards. Keen babies try to lift their head before their neck is strong enough to sustain a steady posture. So they tend to wobble and possibly bang onto your nose when you are holding them close to your face. However, they steadily build stronger muscles by their willingness to keep trying.

Sally Goddard Blythe's observations about babies spending too much time in baby seats – in a car or for convenience in a busy environment – continue to be highly relevant for good practice. There are times when it is wise, and safe, to have a baby secure in a proper seat. They can gain from being able to see what is going on. But they risk losing out on the kind of movement that is possible when they are placed safely on a comfortable surface on the floor.

- Babies and young children have a biological drive to be active. So it takes active discouragement, through unwise adult actions, to stop their lively physical activity.
- Young babies experiment with a wide range of movements, some of which are random and involuntary at the outset. Then repetition means that they begin to build on the unintended consequences of a kick, a wave, a push. They make deliberate actions and you notice more control.
- The more a baby is enabled to move, the more they become able to make their body do what they want. Actual physical action sends messages to the baby's brain and repeated actions become laid down as a neural pathway. 'Do it again' is perfect for brain development and babies are natural repeaters.
- For instance, watch a baby who is keen to repeat actions like reaching out and grabbing, or dropping items. You will notice how quickly they become confident and their actions move smoothly, as well as obvious improvement in coordinating what their eyes see with what their limbs do.

For example

Babies like to be close and they need this warm physical reassurance wherever they are. In the first half of the baby year, they are very dependent on their immediate environment, created by familiar adults. It will be some time before they can get themselves to areas and items of interest.

- Over her early months, Tanith liked to be cuddled up close. She was at ease with the momentum of being moved around against my chest, secure in a baby carrier.
- Like all babies, in the earliest weeks, her movements looked random. Yet she had a firm grip and would hold tight to a finger. By seven to eight weeks Tanith was very active, working on her muscle control and able to move her head. She struggled to move her whole body, and moved her hands and feet vigorously.
- Over her third month her kicking became so vigorous that she was able to kick her baby shawl off her legs. She was now able to shift from a position of lying on her side to her back.
- She liked to be helped in vigorous movements and her first loud, throaty laugh came when, at four to five months, she was enjoying a game with her father. Tanith was laid on her back and Lance lifted her arms up and down in a friendly, repetitive exercise movement.
- Over her fifth month, Tanith was able to bash toys, sometimes off the edge of the tray on her seat. She liked lying on her back on a blanket and developed a two- and one-handed grip for rattles. She also used her fingers to touch and scrabble at anything of interest, including faces.
- Safe on the blanket on the floor, Tanith made determined efforts to roll and twist herself. She perfected a roll from side to side. Placed on her stomach, she made scrabbling movements with her hands and humped her feet.
- In her fifth month Tanith appeared to surprise herself with a roll from lying on her stomach over onto her back. She then repeated herself over the next few days to the point where it looked like a purposeful move.
- By mid-month she had perfected a fairly stable sitting position, although she risked topping over if something of interest caught her attention. Laid on her back, she was able to lift her head, shoulders and upper back off the floor.

Experiencing movement with you

Babies need to have plenty of ordinary, happy experience of recognising the messages of their own body. This proprioceptive feedback – making sense of direct physical sensations – is also active when you create the movement for a baby.

- Long before babies can choose to rock to and fro themselves, they enjoy this sensation, cuddled in your arms, as you rock gently.

Being a helpful adult

Watch a five or six month old secure in a baby seat and then freely moving on the floor.

- What is this baby able to do? What can he or she not do in each environment?
- If you care for babies of this age who have not been brought out of their seat much so far, then do not give up at the first attempt. Being unsecured may feel like an odd sensation to this baby.
- Make sure you are on the floor as well – stretch out for your full length, just like the baby.
- Make this time personal and full of friendly communication.
- You do not necessarily need toys as such; you are the best play equipment in this situation.

- A slightly different rocking movement is possible when you have a baby lying along the upper half of your legs. Depending on your own physical agility, this experience can be easier to provide when you are sitting on a chair of suitable height. The baby's feet are towards your body and you can create a gentle rocking/bouncing motion, as well as moving their arms if they enjoy that. Singing at the same time is optional – watch and see what this baby likes best.
- Long before they can shift their position by bending their knees, let alone jumping, you can give them the up-and-down sensation when you lift them up and down in your arms.
- A baby's key person, and then a few familiar other adults in a nursery, get to know individual babies. Some definitely let you know that they like these movements to be more vigorous than another baby of a similar age. You adjust what you do to the wishes of this baby, which are communicated by their body language and sound making.
- When you dance, with a baby in your arms, he or she experiences the gentle twirls and shifts of perspective – back and forth. Again, individual babies will let you know how lively they like this 'Come dancing' experience to be.

Time on the floor

Babies need to have generous time for their physical explorations. They are finding out all about:

- Where do I end and other people start?
- What's that? Is that my hand, how do I make it work like that?
- Where's it gone now?
- How did I do that? Can I do it again?

They need plenty of time on a comfortable, flat surface such as the floor, made a pleasant place to be by soft coverings and a safe area because you deal with any potential problems of the floor being a thoroughfare for adults or mobile toddlers and young children. Very young babies need to be protected, of course, but they are secure on this comfortable base with you beside them.

- Babies can lie on their back looking up or across at you. If you are close by, then your face and interaction makes this interesting. However, a comfortable place for babies on their back can be made interesting with mobiles, some of which can be created by you – not all bought items.
- Babies experience a variety of sensations from their own body. They are able to wave arms and legs vigorously. They experience a firm, but comfortable base as they wriggle or move their head to and fro. When they are able to squirm and push against the floor, babies are able to lever themselves to the side in ways in that are impossible if they are secure in a baby seat.

When babies are sleeping in their cot, for safety, they should be placed on their back and not their stomach. This advice is supported by research to reduce the risk of unexplained death of infants whilst sleeping in their cot. However, this sound advice about sleeping position is not applicable to when babies are fully awake. Babies, whose muscle control has reached their shoulders, can be placed on their stomachs for short periods of time. These are babies who are now able to lift their face and part of their upper body off the surface. They need plenty of what is sometimes now called 'tummy time'.

- From this position, babies can stretch their legs, arms and spine in safe ways. They are able to strengthen the muscles in their neck and shoulders and continue the progress of increasing control down their body.

- Of course you do not leave babies in this position when they are clearly letting you know they have had enough for now. Again, if you are on the floor with them, then this position does not feel as if they are alone.
- So long as you are close and observant, babies will not become distressed. You will help them before their sound-making communication moves from the message of, 'This is not very easy' to 'I'm really fed up now', or even 'I am in a right fix and I don't like it one bit!'

For example

During my time with the under threes team in Grove House, I watched an older baby who was spending time on his stomach, but was currently unimpressed by this experience.

I lay down full length, on my stomach, facing him. I caught his gaze and slowly lifted my head and shoulders off the floor. He looked interested straight away and reacted with a half smile. I continued to lift and lower myself a couple more times and he began to copy me.

It is easy for us to forget that it can feel a bit boring for a baby placed in the tummy position, unless an adult is very close.

The value of crawling

For babies the value of time on their stomach is also that they are in the right position to get onto all fours, when they have the muscle strength. Sometimes they will manage to roll over from lying on their back. When they try out the all fours position, babies start to take some of their weight on their outstretched hands, as well as their knees and legs. They work their palms in the full stretch that is necessary to hold their weight in this position, then rock to and fro and finally to learn to crawl. This movement of lifting their body weight off the floor is a natural and positive gymnastic game that helps their spine to become more flexible through freedom of movement in the joints, and also builds up strength in their arms and legs.

Even when babies did not spend so much time in baby seats, some of them went straight into walking. However, most babies will spend time crawling, before walking, when they are placed on the floor for generous amounts of time. Of course you do not pressure a baby to crawl before they are ready – their bones and joints need to be strong enough to take their weight. However, even

Being a helpful adult

- Be close and in a similar position on the floor to the baby. Provide company, as well as the example that it is enjoyable to be there.
- Move an object slightly closer to a child to encourage that stretch or effort to move independently. Do not always hand it over, but obviously do not hold back so much that a baby is frustrated or distressed.
- Let babies experience a bit of frustration. A baby who is moved straightaway does not learn to persevere in an attempt to move themselves.
- If a baby is really struggling to get into a forward crawl, then try giving them a firm support by placing your hands against their feet. You do not push the baby; you let the baby push against your hands.
- Be willing to crawl with the child in a game of crawling-chasing, with you sometimes doing the 'chasing' and sometimes being 'chased'. When you crawl with enthusiasm, it is almost as if you are a mobile item of equipment. Toddlers and twos also enjoy going underneath the 'tunnel' you make in an all-fours position, or facing you in a nose-to-nose position.
- Crawl together through a tunnel, if you have one, or under lightweight material, like organza. And do keep going with these lively physical games into the toddler year.

those babies who out of choice look like they are missing out the crawling stage for mobility will still enjoy games of crawling around, so long as you are obviously having fun. In partnership with parents, it is important for you to highlight what babies gain by plenty of crawling time. Deal, if necessary, with the misleading idea that early walking or going straight to walking is a preferable developmental pattern – signs of a 'better', or more impressive, baby.

The great advantage of crawling, as a form of independent mobility, is that it is a total work out for the body, using both sides in a coordinated movement. Watch a crawling baby and you can observe how each side of their body is used in a smooth action, which brings the right arm to move with the left leg and the left arm with the right leg. Once a baby is a confident crawler, this complex, coordinated motion is undertaken with impressive speed.

Babies combine the vital information from their hands, and often also from knees and feet to create a familiar sensation of what crawling feels like. They experience the sense of stillness and of motion. But they also use vision, looking down at the floor sometimes, looking ahead into the distance of the room or across the grass outdoors. They gain valuable experience of checking what they see against where they are and where they plan to reach.

For example

Babies follow a similar, but not identical pattern as they move towards their form of independent mobility.

- By her seventh month, Tanith was able to cover a short distance, starting from lying on her back. A vigorous humping movement meant that she travelled backwards in this way, her face still upwards.
- Placed on her stomach, she was now able to get into the crawling position, although not to make any progress in movement. Her legs were strong and she loved to stand, with her arms held, and to bend her knees in order to bounce and weave about on the spot.
- By her eighth month she was confident in her sitting position and able to twist, lunge for something of interest and return to a stable sitting position ready to explore what she had grabbed.
- She liked very much to seize our outstretched hands and pull herself strongly up to a standing position. She also liked to stand, supporting herself with both hands flat on the low, and very stable, coffee table.
- Over the next few weeks she steadily mastered the ability to pull herself up from a seated position and, over her ninth month, practised the art of cruising along the furniture, shifting her handholds as she went.
- Over her eighth month, Tanith had steadily mastered the business of crawling. At the beginning of the month she could get into the hands-and-knees crawling position and was able to rock herself to and fro vigorously. She would then look up with a surprised expression on her face, as if to say, 'I've done so much moving! Why am I still in the same place?'
- By mid-month she had perfected a kind of combination crawl and stomach squirm. Initially, Tanith succeeded only in moving backwards. Her facial expression and stream of sounds told us clearly that she was very annoyed about this situation.
- Over the next few days her focus on practice was impressive and very soon she managed her first forward crawl. A couple of repetitions and Tanith perfected the style. From then on, she never went backwards, unless that movement was intentional.

For example

During my time in Rainbow, Southland and Grove House, I saw many examples of an encouraging approach by practitioners involved with the very youngest children.

- In all the nurseries, practitioners spent a lot of time sitting on the floor with older babies and young toddlers. Sometimes the sitting was outdoors on a comfortable rug.
- The children were able to move around, with the adults remaining in one place. There were also adult hands at the ready to help and adult shoulders at the right height for older babies to lean and get a hand hold, as they moved from one place to another.
- Very young children need to manage the physical movements for climbing steps – going up and coming back down again. Grove House had an indoor, low level clambering area with an entry either side. Older babies and toddlers were able to take their time crawling or clambering, moving forwards or sometimes preferring to turn around and emerge backwards.

Being a helpful adult

Using hands, knees and legs offers older babies a very efficient way of getting around independently. As some point, toddlers will learn to walk and some of them achieve upright mobility by the end of their baby year or relatively early in the second year of life.

Wherever they spend their time, older babies and toddlers are helped by encouragement, but no pressure towards walking. They need to continue to build their strength, as well as their confidence. To young one-year-olds, the gap between them and the familiar adult can look a wide space. An adult's outstretched hands and fingers close that gap.

Some independent upright mobility starts with a very young one-year-old who can push along a stable trolley. For this action to be successful, they often need an adult who ensures the pathway, indoors or outside, is clear. Other useful adjustments to the environment include well-placed furniture that offers handholds.

Food for thought

Very young babies are 'helpless' in some ways: they cannot feed themselves or get themselves out of trouble. But we misunderstand very early development if we assume they are passive and do not do much at all.

The examples through this section show that babies are highly motivated to help themselves to become more adept and to exercise more and more control over their familiar world. They expend a great deal of energy and dogged perseverance to become a mobile, exploring toddler who makes a difference to his or her own environment.

Physical ways of exploring the world

In the first year of life, babies are motivated to use their current physical skills to the full. At different points over this time, you will notice that a baby has a favourite way of connecting physically with items in their familiar environment. They will persevere in using this skill as the way to learn more about their world. These persistent ways of behaving are called schemas and in the baby year you will observe schemas of physical action rather than the sequences (like transporting items) that become possible in the toddler year and later.

You are likely to observe most, possibly all of these physical schemas over the first year, as babies become more physically adept.

- Mouthing and sucking: babies explore by putting objects to their mouths and continue to use this method into the second year of life. The nerve endings of a baby's lips, mouth and tongue are the most sensitive in their body. So, they are using the most effective means to play and learn.
- Holding: very young babies have to put all their energy into combining vision and stretch to get hold of an interesting object or part of a person. Initially they cannot easily open their grasp to let go again. So, if they have got hold of your hair or that of another child, you often have to undo their grasp. Once they can hold tight to an item of interest, they can also wave it to and fro. (Look at page 35 and 47 for what babies did in the World of Discovery sessions.)
- Inspecting: once babies can hold and look, they often stare at an object of interest. They may look at what appear to be very minor details, but everything is new to them. Continued experience is needed before objects and people become familiar.
- Hitting: babies now have greater physical control and can follow through by looking. So they can connect with an object or substance with more energy. They may tap at a teddy or pat down on a wet surface on their highchair.
- Shaking: the ability to hold tight and then make movement allows babies to move an object from side to side. Perhaps it makes a noise, like a rattle or material cubes with bells inside. Then the pleasure of making something happen encourages babies to

repeat the action. Their physical ability enables them to explore cause-and-effect at a simple and intriguing level.

- Examining: once babies become able to use both hands and to shift their grip, they can examine in detail. Babies become interested in moving an object, taking a close look, and perhaps a poke, from different angles. Babies become more able to manipulate an object so that they can turn or push it around.
- Tearing: babies who manage to explore paper objects may discover the delights of tearing. This action provides a mixture of sound and interesting cause-and-effect. Tearing is often combined with a scrunching and bashing action, which also looks very satisfying to the baby.
- Rubbing: babies become interested in texture and may move a soft toy or piece of material against their cheek or mouth. By bringing the item close to their face, some babies appear to get some more information, as well as enjoy the sensation.
- Dropping: babies' ability to grasp, let go and track with their eyes adds the intriguing possibility of dropping objects. This action is even more interesting to do from a height as that adds a noise.
- Throwing: babies' physical skills continue to develop until they can manage the complex sequence of holding something and then combining the throwing and letting go actions.

Once older babies have achieved physical control over a number of ways to manipulate objects, they no longer restrict themselves to the same physical action or schema. You will notice that they try several different approaches to the same item. They are able to combine different actions in a deliberate sequence, such as grasping hold of something, mouthing it for a while, then turning it around and maybe dropping or throwing it.

For example

In the World of Discovery session (see also page 35), Angie, a 10 month old girl, sat securely for a long time, exploring different items within her reach, one at a time in the order that she chose to pull them into her lap.

- Angie spent a while with a black and white circle with a busy pattern that had been laminated. This resource bent easily in her hands and she was busy waving it about and moving it from one hand to the other.
- Then Angie pulled in a length of white plastic chain, which she rattled and pulled, with a strong hold on different parts of the chain.
- Then she grasped a black quilted oven glove. First she held tight onto the glove, then Angie put it on her head, took it off, shook it well and then threw it.
- She then returned to her investigation of the laminated design. Unexpectedly, it flew out of her hands and Angie moved quickly from her sitting position to a semi all fours to reach out, grasp the laminate, pull it back and settle herself back into the sitting position.
- Later, Angie had the lid of a black and white box and was pretending to give it. That is the only word to use, since Angie gave all the signals that this was a teasing kind of play. She offered the lid to her mother, her mother said 'ta', yet Angie held on tight. The look on her face really did suggest that this action was deliberate. Then Angie repeated the same pattern with another adult.
- Angie did a lot of holding items up to show, seeking acknowledgment from the adults – her mother and then me - before selecting another item. She managed to get her sock off, held it up for my approval and then explored it. Rather like with the oven glove, Angie felt the sock, rubbed it over her head and right to the back of her neck and then back to the front again.

Being a helpful adult

A baby's environment must be clean enough and some items definitely need sterilising. Otherwise, there are disadvantages when adults become obsessed with hygiene. The exception is when a baby or child has chronic health problems that make them especially vulnerable.

There is good reason to be concerned about enthusiastic use of anti-bacterial products on surfaces or in contact with play resources. There is a strong possibility that these are contributing to the level of allergic reactions. Cleaning with soapy water and rinsing is usually enough. You are not trying to reach a medical standard sufficient for doing operations. Furthermore, some of the serious problems in hospitals have rested upon a lack of basic hygiene.

Building healthy habits

Adults are responsible for taking good care of babies and young children and early childhood is the best time to build healthy habits.

- Healthy children need to be physically active, out of choice, and ideas earlier in this section have highlighted that, unless they are prevented, babies are keen to be busy with their hands, legs and whole bodies. It takes seriously unwise adult behaviour to block this physical enthusiasm over the baby and toddler months – let alone to produce sedentary older children who no longer choose to engage in physical play.
- Nutritious food and drink will prime baby and toddler taste buds, without the over stimulation of highly processed foods. Good nutrition, including appropriate drinks, builds healthy bones and fuels growth.
- Sufficient rest and sleep is also important. Like food, you develop healthy routines in partnership with parents. However, you keep a close eye on the limits to continuity with the family home. You will have to talk the issues through with a parent, if you have good reason to be concerned that parents' preference would unbalance their young child's diet or require them to go without a much needed nap.

Important times of nurture definitely reflect good practice for the EYFS and support very young learning. Respect for the personal care of babies and toddlers was discussed in general on page 00. The ability of babies and toddlers steadily to share in their own care is also covered within the context of physical development – because of the skills which babies learn as well as well as holistic health issues.

For example

- In Southlands Crèche, at the same time as Joanne was enjoying a book with one baby (see page 26), Claire was keeping two babies company who were enjoying their lunch. Claire kept her attention on each baby and made it a personal time for each one. She helped them as appropriate and also commented on what they were doing and enjoying eating.
- In Grove House Infant and Toddler, the key person remains close to their key babies and toddlers over mealtimes, including the reality that the younger babies are not necessarily eating at the same time as everyone else. Practitioners feed babies who are unable yet to feed themselves. But the key person looks for the opportunity to provide babies with the means to feed themselves. They are given finger food as appropriate and the encouragement to pick up and get food to their mouth.
- In both settings, the older babies have their own spoon and the chance to get some food in their mouth, supported by the key person also with a spoon. Generous time is given for mealtimes – as an important part of the day and to ensure that there is no temptation to think, 'It's quicker, or less messy if I do it.'

An emotionally warm environment and patient adults will encourage young toddlers to take on some of their own care as well as want to help out generally in a home-like nursery, just as in a family home. Of course, you need to keep them safe, but without blocking this aspect of their growing knowledge and understanding of their world.

Food for thought

Good practice has to be a balance between respect for family preferences and the knowledge of experienced practitioners over what is most likely in the best interests of a baby or toddler – or almost certainly a potential threat to their health and well being.

Childminders, just as much as practitioners in a nursery, need to find a courteous way to explain their reasons for preferring not to follow a food habit from home that is really not a healthy habit. For instance, a wish to establish partnership should not lead you to agree to give sugary drinks to a baby or toddler or to add sweets or crisps to the daily diet, because this child has been allowed to get used to them at home.

Creative Development

Creative development over early childhood is only partly about exploration with arts and crafts, as enjoyable as those opportunities can be. This area of learning and development within the EYFS is about nurturing the flair of creativity in how young children approach flexible play resources and open-ended, first hand experiences.

Creative thinking and exploration

A thoughtful approach to experiences can start in early childhood - long before children are able to put their thoughts into spoken words. The sense of 'what will happen if I...?', 'Will it happen again?' and 'How come that happened?' are building blocks for confident young children. You can observe those events right from the first year of life, as even young babies use their eyes, ears and growing physical skills to make sense of, and act upon, their personal world.

Examples of critical/creative thinking often focus on how you might notice the development, once children have a significant vocabulary and the ability to ask their own questions. However, key messages, right from the first year are that babies, with relaxed time for play and suitable open-ended resources, will build on the experiences they have had so far. So long as they are allowed to be active, to get their hands onto interesting resources, babies make their own connections, try out ideas and repeat actions with their own variations. Babies will show you by facial expression long before they have the words, what they are thinking. Older babies and young toddlers communicate feelings and thoughts that could be worded something like, 'Yes, thought that would happen', 'Now that is interesting, I wasn't expecting that' or 'Hmm, need to try that one again'. Sometimes their expression and slightly tense posture tells you 'I don't like that at all! Who made that happen?', when sometimes it was their action, but baby/toddler understanding of cause-and-effect has a long way to go.

Babies and young toddlers are keen to explore and try out what works in their world. Their open-mindedness gives them a head start in creative development and we need to ensure that our own concerns do not get in the way. Of course you need to keep them safe; babies and toddlers have no sense of personal risk and actual danger. However, a safe enough indoor and outdoor environment will provide plenty of food for thought to nourish infant and toddler brains. You want babies to be keen to find out for themselves, as much from when something does not quite go as planned as when it has gone smoothly. Young children can develop as creative thinkers when they are allowed to make decisions in their play. Also, safety is not only physical; young children need to feel emotionally secure in order to flourish through their creative development.

Creativity means following the flow

The focus in the EYFS on plenty of scope for genuinely child-initiated experiences applies to the whole age range. The play resources for babies and young toddlers will not be exactly the same as for slightly older children, but they have much in common. In order for all young children to exercise choice, they need an attractive learning environment with plenty of accessible materials on open shelves and in containers. Babies will look (or eye-point) to objects of interest and older babies will soon point with a hand or finger. Crawling babies will cross a room or outdoor surface to reach interesting resources and, like mobile toddlers, will often bring together play resources in a creative way.

Being a helpful adult

Early years practitioners sometimes feel that the EYFS Principles into Practice card 4.3, Creativity and Critical Thinking, poses a challenge to understand and put into practice with over threes, let alone in application to babies and young toddlers. It is useful to revisit what is meant by 'critical thinking' and consider what it may look like baby- and toddler-style.

- The term 'criticle thinking' refers to purposeful and reflective judgement around the what, why, when, where and how of relevant experiences.
- Sometimes, the thought process might focus on the 'I wonder...' of prediction and anticipation about what may or will happen. Sometimes it may be about what is going on, trying to get a mental grip on events.
- At other times there may be greater focus on why something has happened, a plausible explanation. Also what does this event or experience mean – how does it connect with what I already know, or do I have to rethink what I thought I knew?

How might you notice this kind of mental hard work from watching the actions of babies and what their facial expression and gestures say to you? Baby and toddler critical thinking in action has a strong dose of 'maybe', 'why not?' and 'here goes!'.

Alert, informal observation helps you to notice the flow of a child's creative enterprises, rather than impose adult reservations about 'proper play'. You need to focus on what actually interests this baby or young toddler today. For instance:

- Sitting babies will spend a long time – surprisingly long to practitioners or parents who say, 'Babies can't concentrate' – when they get their hands into a Treasure Basket (see page 28) or other container of interesting materials, such as a basket full of ribbons or scarves.
- Babies and toddlers puzzle things out in their personal world by getting hold of items, manipulating them and trying things out again and again, or with slight variations of their own choosing. When you watch and listen carefully, you can understand why Alison Gopnik and her colleagues called the US edition of their (1999) book about how very young children think *The scientist in the crib*.
- Toddlers will spend ages playing at making faces in a mirror, hiding and emerging from a large piece of material, or finding out how the world looks through their legs. Look and listen to their discovery play. Let them see you enjoy watching and add a comment, if it seems appropriate.

Food for thought

Older babies and young toddlers show you the power of their creative thinking when they act so as to amuse a familiar adult or children.

- In the second half of their first year, babies will often repeat an action that has made people laugh – one reason you try very hard not to laugh the first time that babies blow out a raspberry sound after food.
- Mobile toddlers, who can control deliberate physical actions, may repeat spontaneous clowning around when it has brought appreciative laughter.
- Young toddlers show a sense of humour, when they deliberately try to make everyone laugh again by the action that worked last time.
- It will be a long time before they can tell a conventional joke. However, some toddlers set out to amuse by saying something they know to be incorrect.

Reflect on the baby and toddler thinking power that lies behind endearing and amusing incidents. Long before they can put it into actual words, they show the ability to observe. They make causal connections between 'what I did' and 'how they reacted', and the intention to repeat that stream of meaningful sounds, those lively gestures or that funny walk.

- Look back at the examples on page 35 and 47 about the World of Discovery sessions. I could just as reasonably have placed that material with creative development.
- There is a lovely sequence in the DVD from Birth to Three Matters, in which an older baby explores what he can do with two balls, including rolling them down the back of a second baby, conveniently sitting close by.

Enthusiasm for doing – in my personal way

Young children cannot learn to be creative, if they are told what they should create. Creativity involves the flair of adding something tangible or an idea - something that is special to you. Older babies and young toddlers relish getting connected with arts and crafts materials. They need to be able to use all their senses and to explore what they can do with materials. Serious blocks to creative development can happen when practitioners are pressurised to get even babies to make something that can be part of a tidy wall display. An even worse case scenario emerges if there is pressure on a baby or toddler room to make something linked with an adult-determined topic followed by the three to fives.

Young creativity is undermined when adults require an end product. Genuine creations need to be chosen and undertaken by children themselves. They decide if they are pleased or irritated with their creation; if it is good enough or fit for the bin. Some practitioners feel a sense of pressure to have something for parents to take home even when the children are babies and young toddlers. Perhaps there is a misplaced concern that sticky pictures or Mother's Day cards are evidence of value for childcare fees. However, many parents will be well aware that their baby or toddler could not possibly have made this neat production.

The sense of pressure may be provoked by parents' comments about, 'Hasn't he done anything today?' For childminders or nurseries, it is usually one or two parents and not everyone. Good practice is to welcome parents' interests but to lead through visual ways to share 'what your baby did today'. Photographs can show the genuine thrill of toddler foot painting and creative piles or collections from a generous store of tubes, shiny pebbles or large corks.

For example

- When I visited the Rainbow Centre in Norfolk, the baby room team had recently created a wall display arising from a painting session with the babies. An array of photos showed babies with their hands and feet fully involved in the paint. The images were arranged around a very large sheet of paper on which many babies had chosen to splosh paint and create marks.
- It was easy for parents to see how much their baby had enjoyed this full-on art experience. Yet there was no misleading message that any baby had made a conventional and finished 'painting'.

This accurate wall display contrasted with mistaken practice I have seen in some other settings, when artwork fixed to the wall or given to parents to take home cannot possibly have been done by the babies or toddlers. The same criticism applies to alleged baby and toddler art, when an adult has obviously cut out all the shapes - babies have not made a 'rocket' or a 'starfish'.

Hands-on creative exploration

Once babies are sitting securely, their hands are free and they love to explore natural materials like water or a thin, sploshy cornflour mix. The Birth To Three Matters DVD has another excellent sequence where a young toddler is sitting up to a Perspex room divider, using hands to swirl paint around on the surface. Genuine creativity develops when young children are enabled to explore and supported by adults who value the doing, the process.

You build firm foundations for young creativity by providing resources and appropriate tools, and then letting babies and young children get their hands onto resources. You are nearby to keep them safe and show an interest.

- Young children need time to explore art and craft materials. For babies, the best tools are their hands and feet and they like to engage very directly with interesting materials.
- Young toddlers like simply to pick up materials and move them about. So long as they have plenty of time to explore the properties of materials, in a few months time they will be more able and interested to use objects as printing tools. A shower scrunchy, feathers or twigs will be brought together with thick paint and large sheets of paper.
- Young toddlers start to explore soft playdough, or other easy to manipulate mixtures. Again, their hands and fingers are their tools and they like to squeeze, poke and push materials around.

The power of imagination

The development of make-pretend is connected to the development of language over very early childhood, and with play behaviour in general. You are unlikely to observe a very young child pretending in play unless they have reached the point when they use some recognisable words. Spoken language is itself a symbolic system: spoken words represent (stand for) familiar people and objects. Pretending is a further example of this young child's ability to represent. The first

Food for thought

Babies and toddlers like to watch. The great advantage of mixed age groups – whether in the home of a childminder or in group provision – is that young toddlers are increasingly interested in what other young children do.

Sharp toddler observation skills and imitation are naturally part of early childhood. So, they begin to watch how a slightly older child – friend or sibling – handles the playdough. Young toddlers can also join in cooking activities and like to handle their own bit of bread dough. They watch what other children do, as you all make buns, biscuits or little cakes. It will not be long before these very young children want to make their own.

pretend play actions are often brief. You can easily miss them, if you are not alert, or feel that play is not 'really pretend' until you see the more lengthy three- and four-year-old version.

However, very young children need to build a firm foundation of understanding how their world works. Their power of imagination rests upon, and leaps off, what they have observed. So a great deal of early pretend play is woven around domestic routines and events. A toddler pretends to be doing something that they have seen a familiar adult do for real. You will most likely see the first signs of pretend within the second year of early childhood, but the emergence of this development is very variable. Some very young toddlers start not only to pretend in relation to themselves, but also move into imaginative play that involves other people or their toys.

For example

By 13 months, Tanith enjoyed games with her brother (almost exactly two years older). Drew did not want to play with his sister all the time. But he seemed to genuinely enjoy a lot of their joint games. He had actively developed these, over the time that Tanith was an older baby and especially once she became a mobile, young toddler.

- They played together in the pretend house we had made from the large box in which our dishwasher had been delivered. The play involved a lot of going in and out through the doorway, flinging themselves on the cushions inside and playing 'here I am' through the windows cut into the side of the house.
- By 15 months Tanith enjoyed being an 'assistant' in play with Drew, that she could not have managed on her own. She was happy handing him lego as he made his constructions – a form of complex creativity that was currently beyond her ability.
- I noticed that she imitated a lot of his pretend play, as well as simple imaginative play with us – 'drinking' from a toy cup and 'feeding' from a toy spoon. By 15-16 months of age Tanith had begun to create her own games and play sequences. She was an active participant in a lot of chase and growling games with Drew, rescue scenarios led by Drew's interest in sharks, and ever longer sequences in the cardboard 'house'.
- However, Tanith now initiated pretend play without any support, for instance a short sequence in which she would pick up her toy phone, give it to me with the indication that I should say something, and then take it back and 'talk' into the receiver herself.
- Tanith developed an enthusiasm for playdough. Initially she just tried to eat it but then watched how Drew played and started to imitate him. She was interested to handle the little rolling pin and try the cutters. She also put little bits into the toy saucepan and offered them to me to eat.
- By 19-20 months Tanith was busy with her own pretend play sequences, although still observant of what Drew did in his play - close beside her on many occasions.
- Tanith had imaginative sequences involving dolls, playing with the tea set, pretend cooking with play dough and she made a 'horse's dinner' with raffia in a plant pot. She also liked dressing up, although not necessarily as anyone in particular.

For example

In Grove House I observed how practitioners took seriously the early signs of even very simple pretend play from toddlers.

- Even a brief offering of a pretend drink met with a genuine response from an adult and a comment about the drink or a request for another. A toddler's expressed interest in the toy animals or a vehicle brought an interested response from an adult and a few words or play action that added a little to what this very young child could express unaided.

- Children were keen on the wooden train that was a permanent part of their outdoor space and could easily sit an adult with eight or ten young children. I watched several times as a child started simple pretend around the train and an adult picked up on the implied suggestion and helped create a journey, with all the appropriate noises. The eldest children in this part of the centre were rising threes and so the adult input was directly relevant to help them to build a slightly more complex pretend scenario.

Ready for rhythm

Babies are born attuned to musical rhythm as well as the sound of the human voice (see also page 12 about infant directed speech). They really do appear to have an innate sensitivity to music and tuneful singing – that is to say they are born with this ability. In the final months before birth, babies can hear sounds from 'outside' and they show a reaction of familiarity to songs that they can only have heard while 'inside'. This evidence of learning prior to birth does not, however, support the biased advice of companies who argue that pregnant women can build brainy babies by playing their range of CDs.

Babies and very young children are alert to musical rhythms, the sound patterns of songs, nursery rhymes and different kinds of music. You are the best source of singing and babies will never criticise the quality of your voice.

- Build on the trills of sound that babies make spontaneously, as they move from single sound-making into repetitive, self-made tunefulness. Repeat back some of the baby's sound streams and see them smile.
- Sing to even very young babies and you will notice how they soon recognise a familiar song or rhyme. Watch how their body looks alert, how they grin when they hear the opening notes.
- Be ready to comfort an uneasy or fretful baby or toddler with tuneful humming. This merging of gentle talk and

Being a helpful adult

Toddlers start to exercise real imagination through brief actions. Their play then swiftly develops, so long as they have time to explore and plenty of open-ended play resources. It is important that practitioners recognise these actions as blossoming creativity.

- A toddler of 15-16 months may use a toy spoon to pretend to feed herself. You can see she is pretending, because it is not mealtime and she is chortling.
- Her actions and broad grin communicate, 'You know, that I know, that you know: this is all just pretend!'
- Toddlers pretend with resources that they see used in daily life, like speaking on the toy telephone. You support their imagination by joining in when invited to have a chat on the phone.
- Toddlers may create the vroom-vroom noises for a car and 'fly' a toy aeroplane. Soon you will see that older toddlers can even pretend that a wooden block is a car and 'drive' it along with the correct noises.

semi-singing can be very reassuring to a baby or young child, often combined with gentle rocking in the cradle of your arms or your lap.

- Peaceful singing and lullabies are not only positive for babies. Days with very young children are physically and emotionally tiring. A time to sit in peace, stroking or rocking a young toddler and singing is also relaxing for the adult.
- Suitable songs for older babies and toddlers often come with hand movements, whether done by the singer or gently done to the child. You can also fine-tune any song that a baby or toddler likes with your own special bounces, tickles or helping the baby with arm or leg movements. You come equipped with all that is necessary: arms to hold gently but securely, a firm lap and bendy knees.
- You get to know individuals, so of course you adjust the liveliness to what you now know this baby relishes. In their baby year, both Drew and Tanith were very keen on their father's unique and physically lively versions of 'Is you is, or is you ain't my baby' and 'Robin Hood'.
- Be ready to repeat favourites many times and realise that, once you have added the new movements you have to recall them in detail. This pattern is now an essential part of the song, as far as this baby or toddler is concerned.
- Once a song, rhyme or piece of music becomes familiar, young toddlers will make their own request by word or gesture. Soon they will sing parts of the song.
- Young children are very open-minded, they like anything you sing with enthusiasm and obvious enjoyment: nursery rhymes, popular current songs or older songs like 'Daisy Daisy'.
- Occasionally, with slightly older children, you may all enjoy singing along to a CD. However, a good rule of thumb is that songs emerge from the mouth of a real person attached to a familiar face.

Practitioners and parents do not have to hold to an identical repertoire. However, it is valuable to have a two-way share over the favourites of a baby or toddler: the special gestures as well as the words. Extend your repertoire by asking for family favourites from children's parents. Do not be in a rush to provide songs or music from traditions that are unknown to any of all the children in your care. Very young children need to become familiar with their own cultural tradition and traditions of 'my friend's family'.

It is unwise practice to organise planned sit-down circle imes with a lot of babies and toddlers. (See also the comment on page 17.) In a nursery or a drop-in for parents, you may have a time of adult and baby or toddler singing together. If so, then the timing and length of the session need to be flexible and babies and toddlers need to be on someone's lap, or snuggled up close. It is still usually much more effective to have very small groups.

Making and enjoying music

Young children explore ways to make sounds by using simple tools including their own bodies. Babies soon produce their own trills of sound and discover the fun of blowing raspberries. Playful adults (or older children) join in and very young children soon realise that they come equipped with the best instrument of all - their own voice.

- Older babies and toddlers explore hitting and tapping by using the traditional wooden spoon and saucepan approach. They soon have the co-ordination to make sounds through shaking something. They make scraping sounds with their own nails, but toddlers can be adept with a stick run along railings or the fence.
- You do not need complex musical instruments. You can buy very simple sound makers, basic xylophones, musical shakers and small drums that can tapped by little hands.

Being a helpful adult

Singing and rhymes, like stories, should frequently be a personal experience for babies and any young children – a time when there is an opportunity for snuggling into a familiar adult. With babies, especially younger babies, many of these spontaneous times will be one-to-one or at most one-to-two. Toddlers and young children sit on your lap or cuddle up close.

Recall the emotionally warm sequence in the *Birth to Three Matters* DVD of a practitioner singing with a few children, one of whom is in her lap and the others are leaning up close. This singing time is happening outdoors and looks very relaxed.

- But you can also make your own 'instruments', using cardboard tubes or plastic bottles with different substances securely inside. You can organise outdoor sound systems by fixing up small pots and pans or CDs on a washing line. Or use a wooden frame, like an old-fashioned clothes horse. Provide simple tools and batons for hitting the pans.

Some special sessions may be supported by someone with additional musical experience. The aim should always be that the regular carers are learning ideas, and the confidence, to extend their repertoire.

For example

While I was working with the Grove House Infant and Toddler team, the whole centre was benefiting from regular times with a music specialist. Practitioners with the under threes experienced new songs and music making. They were able to observe which possibilities the children appeared to like the best, so these could become part of the usual day. Special sessions will backfire if practitioners (or parents attending a drop-in) believe that singing and music making is an expert task, to be run only by a specialist.

Babies and toddlers benefit from hearing a range of music played from CDs. Start with what will be more familiar to you and to these individual children's family background and then edge

Food for thought

Young children do not benefit from non-stop background music. It certainly is not 'stimulating' for their creative development; it just becomes sound wallpaper that children have to filter out in order to concentrate.

Nor is it true that certain kinds of classical music boosts babies' intelligence - the so-called Mozart Effect. Wolfgang Amadeus Mozart wrote some excellent music and he can be one of your sources for European classical music. However, his music does not work IQ-magic anymore than an enjoyable CD from Celtic or South American traditions.

outwards. See what you all tune into – patterns of musical tradition vary around the world and adult ears are more attuned to familiar tones and patterns.

Very young children are open-minded in their musical tastes and they certainly do not need exclusively 'children's music', such as songs or theme tunes from age-appropriate DVD or television programmes. You can use this source for some music, especially if you realise from a toddler's reaction that they like this tune - just not as your main source of tunes and songs. It will be a while before babies and young toddlers are able to request particular songs or pieces of music. However, you will notice by their facial expression, and sometimes by their dancing movements, that they recognise a familiar tune.

Most babies like to be danced in your arms and a wise adult gets to know how energetically this baby likes to be jigged. Much like physical play, some babies like it very lively and others prefer a more gentle sway. Once babies are secure on their feet and able to lean against a stable support like a table, some are keen to move to music by swaying themselves from side to side or up and down, by bending their knees. From nine months of age my daughter, Tanith, was an enthusiastic dancer using this style of movement for any kind of lively music.

A love of stories

Babies and toddlers enjoy sharing books and the telling of stories. Soon they indicate clearly that they wish you to read or tell a particular story. Young children need to have their request met at the time they ask, unless there is a very good reason for you to have to postpone. Under threes, and many over threes too, need their story telling in very small groups – a sofa full. It is a personal experience that then connects with their own lived experience.

You will see how toddlers can follow a simple pattern in a story. Your words and gestures provoke their developing imagination and they like to repeat their favourites again and again. The repetition helps young children to learn and then recognise familiar stories. Toddlers start to chime in with repeated lines and have a go at the gestures. You will start to hear toddlers tell stories to themselves using parts of your phrases, even your intonation. So, it is important to tell a story in the same way each time, or with only very minor changes. Young children like to have familiar stories told 'properly'. Their facial expressions and words start to communicate not only, 'what will happen next?', but also 'when will we get to the bit I like about….?'

Babies and young toddlers are at the early stages of a long learning journey towards literacy skills that will eventually be recognised by adults as 'proper' reading and writing. However, their early literacy skills are supported by adults who understand the process and do not try to rush very young children. (See also page 22).

- Communication, language and literacy intermingles with creative development because these very early firm foundations towards literacy include a love of stories and books – right from the baby year.
- Songs and rhymes support babies existing skills of sound making and continue the process of attuning their hearing to the sounds of their familiar language(s).
- Enthusiastic mark making joins with a pleasure in decisions over what goes where. Older babies and young toddlers relish big scale movements and getting their hands into materials that can be swirled, pulled across paper and sloshed onto a surface.

What should concern you?

There is great variation between young children and much will happen although in different patterns, over their baby and toddler year. Practitioners, who care for babies and toddlers, have an important role to support mothers and fathers, if they seem unduly concerned and to help with realistic expectations. Some parents can become enmeshed with direct competition of, 'My baby can... hasn't yours yet?'

Perhaps this other baby has walked at nine or ten months, but that is early for this visually obvious milestone. It will be some months before anyone should be concerned over a mobile older baby or young toddler whose physical independence does not yet include steady walking. It is a different matter if you have an older baby who shows little or no interest in trying to move at all. There is absolutely no benefit to a baby in trying to fast-track the shift into upright walking. There are also disadvantages if adult pressure has zoomed them through an enthusiastic crawling phase (see page 43).

It is within normal range that babies are active with their hands, as well as their eyes. They should steadily be trying to grasp and handle items they can reach. You should be concerned if older babies do not seem to be able to connect with items or their physical skills are not becoming more sophisticated, as described on page 43. It is usual that they imitate actions and sounds that are within their capabilities. So it should concern you if a baby or young toddler is unresponsive to the actions of familiar others. In a similar way it should catch your attention if older babies and young toddlers do not show that they have a growing understanding of their own personal world. People and places should have become familiar and young toddlers should show they know what to do with common items for their play or domestic routines.

It is most unlikely that the nine month 'prodigy' is actually talking in words that anyone else can understand. However, you should be concerned over young babies who do not make sounds or respond at around three to four months to a give-and-take of adults words and baby sound making. In the normal course of events, babies are socially responsive: they show awareness of their immediate surroundings, an interest in human faces and an alertness to the sounds of human speech. Over the first year of life you should notice an increased enthusiasm for sound-making and for social interaction. Over the second year of life, you would expect toddlers' expressive communication to become more like the sounds of speech and for recognisable words to appear. Familiar adults – parents and practitioners – need to be alert for babies who do not react and toddlers who seem socially uninterested. It can be hard to assess sight and hearing for babies, especially if the loss is partial. However, familiar carers can be the first to realise that this baby does not react to what you say unless s/he can see you too.

Further Resources

Accessing materials about the Early Years Foundation Stage (EYFS)

The EYFS applies to England and has been statutory (under the Childcare Act 2006) since September 2008 for all registered provision, including those providers who previously did not take the 'educational' funding and as such were inspected under 'care'.

The EYFS materials are provided within a pack entitled *The Early Years Foundation Stage – Setting the Standards for Learning, Development and Care for children from birth to five*. This pack includes:

- Two booklets: the *Statutory Framework* which describes what is required and, in some cases, what must not be done, and the *Practice Guidance*, which offers a considerable amount of explanation, description and ideas for practice. There is choice about how practitioners draw on this second, longer booklet to support their work. The *Practice Guidance* is not a statement of what you have to do, except those sections which repeat parts of the *Statutory Framework*.
- The single set of Welfare Requirements are in the Statutory booklet.
- The Practice booklet includes the birth to five years descriptive developmental material and suggestions for good practice.
- A poster about the EYFS – led through the four broad, guiding themes of A Unique Child, Positive Relationships, Enabling Environments and Learning and Development.
- A set of twenty four Principles into Practice cards, which provide key ideas and examples about good practice. The Statutory booklet makes it clear that these materials are central for guiding good practice.
- A CD Rom, which includes all the main materials. This resource also provides briefing papers, website links and a series of brief video excerpts.

All providers need to ensure that they have the second edition of the pack, published in May 2008, since there are some corrections, changes and additions from the first edition. EYFS materials can be ordered from DfES Publications tel: 0845 60 222 60 -reference number 00266-2008BKT-EN. Materials are also on: http://nationalstrategies.standards.dcsf.gov.uk/

This website is now the location of many guidance documents for early years and the older age ranges.

Books and websites

- Blythe S G (2004) *The Well Balanced Child: Movement and Early Learning*. Hawthorn Press
- Blythe S G (2008) *What Babies and Children Really Need: how Mothers and Fathers Can Nurture Children's Growth for Health and Well Being*. Hawthorn Press
- Campbell R (1999) *Literacy from Home to School: Reading with Alice*. Trentham Books
- Close R *Television and Language Development in the Early Years: a Review of the Literature* www.literacytrust.org.uk/Research/TV.html (accessed 12/11/2009)

- Community Playthings (2005) *Creating Places for Birth to Three: Room Layout and Equipment* http://www.communityplaythings.co.uk/resources/booklets/creating-places.html (accessed 12/11/2009)
- David T et al (2003) *Birth to three matters: a review of the literature compiled to inform the framework to support children in their earliest years.* DFES: London www.dcsf.gov.uk/research/data/uploadfiles/RR444.pdf (accessed 19/11/09)
- Department for Children Schools and Families (2008) *Every Child a Talker: Guidance for Early Language Lead Practitioners.* DCSF http://nationalstrategies.standards.dcsf.gov.uk/node/153355 (accessed 12/11/09)
- Dorman H, Dorman C (2002) *The Social Toddler: Promoting Positive Behaviour.* The Children's Project
- Early Childhood Unit *Everyday Stories* (Descriptive observations from the research undertaken of under threes in day nurseries during the mid-1990s by Peter Elfer and Dorothy Selleck.) Accessible via www.everydaystories.org.uk (accessed 12/11/09)
- Edwards A G (2002) *Relationships and Learning: Caring for Children from Birth to Three.* National Children's Bureau
- Elfer P (2005) Observation Matters. In: Abbott L, Langston A. eds *Birth to Three Matters: Supporting the* Selleck D (2003) *Key Persons in the Nursery: Building Relationships for Quality Provision.* David Fulton
- Featherstone S, ed (2008) *Again, Again: Understanding Schemas in Young Children.* Featherstone Education
- Goldschmied E, Jackson S (2005) *People under Three: Young Children in Day Care* Routledge
- Gopnik A, Meltzoff A, Kuhl P (1999) *How Babies Think.* Weidenfeld and Nicolson
- Gopnik A (2009) *The philosophical baby.* Bodley Head. Also a conversational feature on www.edge.org/3rd_culture/gopnik09/gopnik09_index.html (accessed 12/11/2009)
- Healy J (2004) *Your Child's Growing Mind: Brain Development and Learning from Birth to Adolescence.* Broadway
- Hope S, McTavish A (2007) *A Nurturing Environment for Children up to Three.* Islington Primary Strategy Early Years Team
- Hughes A (2006) *Developing Play for the Under 3s: The Treasure Basket and Heuristic Play.* David Fulton
- Karmiloff-Smith A (1994) *Baby it's You: a Unique Insight into the First Three Years of the Developing Baby.* Ebury Press
- Learning and Teaching Scotland – the early years section www.ltscotland.org.uk/earlyyears/sharingpractice/0-3/index.asp (accessed 12/11/2009)
- Learning and Teaching Scotland (2005) *Birth to Three: Supporting our Youngest Children.* Learning and Teaching Scotland or accessible via www.ltscotland.org.uk/earlyyears/about/birthtothree/guidance.asp (accessed 12/11/2009)
- Lindon J (2005) *Understanding Child Development: Linking Theory and Practice.* Hodder Arnold
- Lindon J (2006) *Helping Babies and Toddlers Learn: A Guide to Good Practice with Under Threes.* National Children's Bureau
- Lindon J (2006) *Care and Caring Matter: Young Children Learning through Care.* Early Education
- Lindon J (2006) A sofa full of talkers. In: Featherstone S, ed *L is for Sheep: Getting Ready for Phonics.* Featherstone Education
- Lindon J (2008) *Safeguarding Children and Young People: Child Protection 0-18 years.* Hodder Arnold
- Lindon J (2009) *Parents as Partners: Positive Relationships in the Early Years.* Practical Pre-School Books

- Lindon J, Kelman K, Sharp A (2008) *Play and Learning in the Early Years: Practical Activities and Games for the Under 3s.* Practical Pre-School Books
- Manning-Morton J, Thorp M (2006) *Key Times: a Framework for Developing High Quality Provision for Children under Three Years Old.* Open University Press
- Murray L, Andrews L (2000) *The Social Baby: Understanding Babies' Communication from Birth.* CP Publishing
- National Literacy Trust – useful website with plenty to download, www.literacytrust. co.uk link to valuable www.talktoyourbaby.org.uk and reviews of developments like baby signing www.literacytrust.org.uk/talktoyourbaby/signing.html (all accessed 12/11/2009)
- Oates J, ed (2007) *Attachment Relationships – Quality of Care for Young Children.* Bernard Van Leer Foundation or via www.bernardvanleer.org (accessed 19/11/09)
- Pawl J (2006) Being held in another's mind. In: Lally JR, Mangione P, Greenwald D, eds, *Concepts for Care: 20 Essays on Infant/Toddler Development and Learning.* Wested. Also accessible via www.wested.org/online_pubs/ccfs-06-01-chapter1.pdf (accessed 12/11/2009)
- Tayler C (2007) The brain, development and learning in early childhood. In: *Understanding the Brain: the Birth of a Learning Science.* Centre for Educational Research and Innovation : 161 – 183. Also accessible via www.dcsf.gov.uk/research/ data/uploadfiles/DCSF-RW030.pdf (accessed 12/11/2009)
- TLRP *Neuroscience and Education: Issues and Opportunities – a Commentary by the Teaching and Learning Research Programme* (www.tlrp.org/pub/documents/Neuroscience20% Commentary20% FINAL.pdf)
- Trevarthen C et al (2003) *Meeting the Needs of Children from Birth to Three.* research review – download a summary on www.scotland.gov.uk/Publications/2003/06/17458/22696 or the full report on www.scotland.gov.uk/Resource/Doc/933/0007610.pdf (both accessed 19/11/09)
- Zeedyk S (2008) *Do Baby Buggies Affect Development?* National Literacy Trust. Also accessible via http://www.literacytrust.org.uk/talktoyourbaby/pushchairs_research. html (accessed 19/11/09)

DVDs

- Beckmann Visual Publishing Baby *It's you: the First Three Years.* Six programmes from the Channel 4 series and an extra programme about early brain development www. beckmanndirect.com (accessed 12/11/09)
- Early Education *Supporting Young Children's Sustained Shared Thinking: an Exploration and Exploring Young Children's Thinking through their Self-chosen Activities* (DVD and booklets by Marion Dowling) www.early-education.org.uk (accessed 12/11/09)
- National Children's Bureau *Infants at Work: Babies of 6-9 Months Exploring Everyday Objects, Heuristic Play with Objects: Children of 12-20 Months Exploring Everyday Objects* (Elinor Goldschmied and Anita Hughes) www.ncb.org.uk (accessed 12/11/09)
- Siren Film and Video Ltd *The Wonder Year, Attachment and Holistic Development: the First Year, Exploratory Play, Firm Foundations for Early Literacy and Supporting Early Literacy* www.sirenfilms.co.uk (accessed 12/11/09)
- Sure Start *Birth to Three Matters: a Framework to Support Children in their Earliest Years* 2002 (The written framework has been replaced by the EYFS, but the good practice shown in the DVD has not changed.)
- The Children's Project *The Social Baby and The Social Toddler* www.childrensproject. co.uk and www.socialbaby.com (both sites accessed 12/11/09)

I have learned a great deal by running training days and leading conferences on good practice with babies and very young children. A heartfelt thank-you for the opportunity to listen and talk with a considerable number of early years practitioners, local advisers and college tutors. In connection with this book, I am especially grateful for the welcome offered by:

- Fran Connell and her team at the Southlands Kindergarten and Crèche, Newcastle-under-Lyme – especially Joanne Gallimore and Claire Hollins who run the baby room.
- Dee Gent and her team at the RAF Marham Rainbow Centre near Kings Lynn.
- Himisha Patel, head of Grove House Children's Centre, Southall and the team of the Infant and Toddler Centre.
- Debbie Shepherd, 0-3s Development Officer, Thurrock – for our conversations about babies and very young children and my visit to The Flagship Centre, Sure Start Tilbury. With thanks to Donna Fletcher for welcoming me to a World of Discovery session for babies with their parents.
- The Charlton Childminders Network, especially Carole Allen and Ellen Edwards.
- Alexa Gilbert, the under 3s unit, Pound Park Children's Centre, Charlton, South London.
- The Greenwich Early Years Advisory Team, in particular Liz Buck, who with Lucy Nettleton, has developed the Forest School project across the borough.

I would also like to thank the following people and teams, whose ideas on early years practice have been so valuable:

- Peter Elfer (senior lecturer, University of Surrey at Roehampton).
- The development team at Community Playthings, especially Martin Huleatt, Helen Huleatt and Martin Rimes.
- Early years advisory teams from Derby, Coventry, Hammersmith and Fulham, and Gloucester.
- The What Matters to Children team, of which I am a member, for what I have learned about the central importance of first-hand experiences.

I have changed the names of any children from examples observed in actual settings. I have retained the names used in published material which I have referenced with brief examples. Drew and Tanith are my own (now adult) son and daughter and they have given permission for me to quote from the individual diaries I kept of their first five years.